I0824326

MY BAD

A Personal History of the Queer Nineties and Beyond

HUGH RYAN

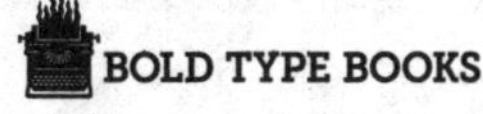

BOLD TYPE BOOKS

New York

Bold Type Books
Hachette Book Group
1290 Avenue of the Americas, New York, NY 10104
www.boldtypebooks.org
@BoldTypeBooks

Printed in the United States of America

First Edition: May 2026

Published by Bold Type Books, an imprint of Hachette Book Group, Inc. Bold Type Books is a co-publishing venture of the Type Media Center and Hachette Book Group, Inc.

The Hachette Speakers Bureau provides a wide range of authors for speaking events. To find out more, go to hachettespeakersbureau.com or email HachetteSpeakers@hbgusa.com.

Bold Type books may be purchased in bulk for business, educational, or promotional use. For more information, please contact your local bookseller or the Hachette Book Group Special Markets Department at special.markets@hbgusa.com.

The publisher is not responsible for websites (or their content) that are not owned by the publisher.

Print book interior design by Amy Quinn.

Library of Congress Control Number: 2025039082

ISBNs: 9781645030577 (hardcover), 9781645030591 (ebook)

LSC-C

Printing 1, 2026

To my parents, my closest allies, for all that we've made it through.

Contents

Introduction

WHEN I WAS SIXTEEN, I DREADED MORE THAN ANYTHING the sound of Sheryl Crow lazily telling her band to "hit it," before a drunken guitar lick launched into "All I Wanna Do," her first number one song.

"All I Wanna Do" was everywhere in 1994, but I mostly remember it as the inescapable soundtrack to my nightly cruise down the information superhighway. I had no stereo yet, just a tinny little radio with a hard-to-tune dial, so it took a lot to commit to changing the station. We'd just gotten a second phone line for my father's work, and after business hours, I had it all to myself. Three things happened every night that year: I logged on, I jerked off, and I yelled at Sheryl Crow to shut the fuck up. Her whiny refrain about having fun cut right through my sexual fantasies, but the radio was across the room and my hands were busy, so I probably listened to that song a thousand times over the course of high school.

The cruelest betrayal of my body in middle age is not my softening belly or fading eyesight but the primordial joy that sparks in me when I hear Sheryl Crow now. I was a scared, sad, closeted teen, but my nervous system remembers only that I was strong, that the world was opening for me pixel by pixel, and that Sheryl was right there next to me, crooning her static-y song of alcoholic joy. And it's not just her: "Tubthumping," "Santeria," even the fucking "Macarena" lights me up these days.

Nostalgia's one powerful motherfucker.

I've been thinking about it a lot recently. Nostalgia. It's the inevitable consequence of watching my adolescent years—the Nineties—repackaged and sold back to me in books, movies, and TV shows. Give me a Daria reference, a Delia's look, and a Snoop D-O-Double-G song, and I'm a happy boy.

Until my brain kicks in. That cunty little killjoy. *What the fuck is this?* it demands, whenever some Nineties repro hits my screen. It's not about the hair, though it's never bleached and gelled crispy enough. Or the eyebrows, which are never penciled in the way they should be, thin as Kate Moss's wrists. The soundtracks are always rad, the flannels are always flannelling, and the modem always screams at just the right pitch.

No, it's the gays. The gays. The endless fucking gays. They traipse lighthearted through the world. They're out to all their friends. No one ever hurts them, or if they do, they apologize before the end of the episode. Their besties are never casually homophobic. They have supportive parents and romantic partners, and they know themselves so well.

Bullshit, my brain snorts.

But I get it. Homophobia's a drag. It's far more comfortable to relegate it to some offstage disembodiment than to let it live in the mouths and fists of characters we're supposed to love. But without it, queer lives don't make any sense. Our flights, our fights, our feral nature—all of that is enervated when we refuse to acknowledge the ubiquitous cruelty of the late last millennium.

When I talk to queer teens now, and they tell me they long for the '90s, I think, *We've failed you*. We've let the guilty erase themselves from history. And that includes us. *Me*. I think about all the mistakes I made, and the people I hurt, as I tried to untwist myself from the knot those years tied me into. We want the past without the pain. But you know what that is?

Disney history; a saccharine fairy tale.

Growing up queer in the '80s and '90s was like living through a war most people never noticed. For a long time, I've wanted to refuse that history—to somehow be unscathed by the very forces that created me. But I'm the product as much of my pain as of my resistance to it. Without one, the other doesn't exist. I watched the world change, and if I can't acknowledge the worst, I can't show you the best either.

The Nineties were hard. And easy, in their way. We had America's last analog childhoods: disconnected, unsurveilled, and free. We were isolated from other queer people, but we were safe from the harsh glare of social media. Our triumphs and failures, shared only with those around us, were quickly forgotten. Our parties were epic, and since there are almost no photographs, no one can contradict me when I say that. It was the last time "selling out" was an insult, not a goal. When the world ended at your door, instead of always being in your pocket. When it was cool not to care about anything or try too hard, because America was *the* global superpower, and even the laziest slacker was going to make it rich off the internet, which we all knew was the future (even though we didn't really know what it was).

Queers of my generation lived through two interconnected sea changes: the explosion of the internet, which gave us both vital community and vital anonymity, and the post-AIDS mainstreaming of American homosexuality, which paradoxically both destroyed and enlarged the worlds we came out into.

We were the last to inhabit the vast gay ghettos and the first to have gay marriage as a viable option. But the further we entered the mainstream, the less of ourselves we gave to those private spaces that nurtured us (and the generations that came before us). It was a necessary trade-off. And by that, I don't mean it was a perfect choice; it was *necessary* in that one could not be done without the other. Only now, in hindsight, can we truly see what we got for what we gave. In the future, the 1990s will be seen as *the* inflection point—the moment when everything changed.

Increasingly, we're in a world where twentieth-century ideas about what it means to be lesbian, gay, bisexual, or transgender can't fully describe the queer community. If a cis man is attracted to cis and trans women, is he straight? What if he's only attracted to trans women or only to cis women? What does it mean if you're attracted to nonbinary people? What if the specific sexual activity you're engaged in matters more to you than the gender of your partners? What if you want to have genitals that aren't congruent with your overall lived gender? Are these "identities" or "fetishes," and who gets to decide?

For a century or so, we've been told that L, G, B, and T are the categories that explain our sexual existence. We might fight over who goes where (especially when discussing historical figures who lived before those terms were defined), but rarely do we think about why these categories exist overall.

Here's the truth I've learned from decades of studying queer history: In the late nineteenth century, America urbanized, allowing queer people to find each other in greater and greater numbers. In turn, a group of largely straight White men studied their lives and writings and decided that sexual object choice and binary gender identification were the essential characteristics that determined who was normally gendered and who was sexually strange. Why? Because those things were easy to observe from a straight perspective, outside the community.

But those slim data points tell us very little about the *experience* of queer desire—they only describe *what* we want, not the *how* and *why* of wanting it. They're useful bits of information, but recently I think they've been holding us back. They're not wrong or bad ideas; they're just limited and derived from a time when we lived very differently.

Only now, as Gen Z (the first fully postinternet generation) is entering adulthood, are we getting a glimpse of queer life beyond L, G, B, or T. As of February 2025, about 23 percent of

Gen Z identified somewhere under the queer umbrella, as did 14 percent of Millennials. That's a massive jump from Gen X's anemic 5 percent. What accounts for this?

It's the downstream effect of our going online and coming out in the 1990s.

In 1995, the Pew Research Center asked about internet usage for the first time and found that only 14 percent of Americans were online; by 2014, that number was over 80 percent. As a result, more people have access to queer ideas and role models at earlier ages and in more places. But it's not just a numbers game. The internet is changing how we understand queerness on a base level.

On the internet, the essential experience of queer identity is through words. Young queer people are much more likely to encounter queer ideas, spaces, sex, and people digitally before they ever do in real life. But they have to describe themselves and the things they're looking for before they can find them. This has pushed them to focus on both what they share with other queer people who have the same sexual object choice or gender identity and what is different between them. To parse out all the many ways one could be bisexual, or transgender, or intersex, or lesbian. To ask questions like, What if all gay people aren't the same, or all trans people, or all bi people? What if, over time or in different situations, our desires—or our selves—can change? What if we understood "sexuality" and "gender" not as separate static circles but as a collection of lanes we could occupy (and sometimes switch between) on a giant highway of desire we're all driving down over the course of our lives?

The internet changed everything, and I was there as it did, logging on, jerking off, and yelling at Sheryl Crow. I didn't understand what was happening at the time. But as I began my career as a queer historian, I realized that the '90s weren't the first time this kind of massive change had happened in American history. The creation of the L-G-B-T model for sexuality was itself a pushback against earlier ideas, spurred on by urbanization instead of the internet. For my first book, *When Brooklyn Was Queer,* I researched how moving into cities changed American ideas about sexuality in the late nineteenth and early twentieth centuries. I was struck by a statistical parallel. In 1800 about 6 percent of Americans lived in cities, by 1900 it was 40 percent, and today it's 80 percent—about the same as the percentage of Americans who are now online. I was tracking two very similar revolutions in queer life—and thus queer identity: one a hundred years before I was born and one that I had lived through.

Queer people are a part of the world we come from; when that world changes, we change with it. This renegotiation is a constant process. In other words, the transformation we're going through right now is unpredictable and world shaking. But not unprecedented. And I think the best way to understand it is to look backward, to examine where we came from and how we got here.

No—where *I* came from and how *I* got here. I lived it, and this is my story to tell, though I've been shirking that responsibility for years, tongue-tied by the ghosts of the homophobia I grew up with, in, despite, and through. The long tail of the '90s has me by the throat, and I'm not alone in that. Our world and our selves were radically transformed by the last decade of the last century, and only now are we beginning to grapple with who we have become in the aftermath. To understand America today, it's essential that we understand the queer Nineties.

For my entire life, I've been spit-roasted by history, sandwiched between two poles: public and private; communal and individual; what to share and what to hide. This is my attempt at a true accounting, written for everyone who was there, everyone who is no longer here, and everyone who never got to see the world we once had.

If I got it wrong, well . . . my bad.

The Last Analog Childhood

SEÑORA WAS MY FAVORITE TEACHER FOR THE FIRST HALF of seventh grade, one of the few who didn't seem to hate spending her wild and precious days getting tweens to care about something. She had us write skits where the characters from *Beverly Hills, 90210* inexplicably found reasons to discuss our *vocabulario* words, every girl doing her best Shannen Doherty (RIP), pulling on a scrunchy and asking, "Don-DE ES-ta el presiDENTe?" Our other teachers were old, ancient, *forty*; Señora did a Mariah Carey impression that was fully off-key but got the essence of her. (In that, she was my early training for understanding drag.)

It was 1990 in Irvington, New York, a sleepy town on the outskirts of New York City where my parents and their extended Bronx Irish clan had landed post White flight. My middle school Spanish class had maybe fifteen students total, and we'd all known each other since kindergarten, to our great regret.

In elementary school, I mostly had incidental friends—neighbors, classmates, or the children of familial acquaintances. With the transition to middle school, they peeled away. I remember sixth grade mostly as a procession of phone calls where embarrassed parents made obvious excuses for why their sons couldn't come to the phone right now, or ever again. It was a little like being dead, and I haunted our cold, brick middle school like a scrawny ghost in a ginormous Ocean Pacific T-shirt that read, "Surf Legend: Gateway to the Sun."

(Why did I own that shirt? The closest I'd been to a surfboard was getting tangled up in a buoy and nearly drowning on the Jersey shore when I was ten.)

Other kids were rarely mean to me because the school punching bag—Booger—was in almost all the same classes I was. When that mob energy whipped up and the playground became a school of piranhas looking for something to eat, we usually turned on Booger. Yes, *we*; I'd have done anything to be part of something. I kicked that kid because he was lower than I was, a smudge on my soul that will never come out. But it got me nowhere, because shared hatred is not the same as friendship; it just sings in the same key for a minute.

So perhaps I was particularly open to Señora's kindness, but we were all a little ensorcelled by her. Other teachers wanted *us* to like *them*, but we all wanted *her* to like *us*.

She listened to us—not our *feelings*; it was 1990, no one cared about that shit. But Señora eavesdropped on our conversations and found ways to work Nintendo and Vanilla Ice into our lessons ("Yo, yo, yo means I, I, I"). That's how it all started, on a gray day in late fall or early winter. I have a hard time remembering the rest of that year, and as I've grown older, that block has worked its way backward, devouring the seventh grade quiz by quiz and week by week, leaving a few unforgettable moments bobbing unmoored in an indistinct ocean.

It was cold, I remember that, and Stevie C. was being a little shit. He was one of those kids who never came at you directly but was always talking smack just loud enough for you to hear. As we settled into our metal chairs with desks attached and waited for the bell to ring, he kept up a steady string of gay jokes directed at the air around me: "Know what GAY stands for? Got AIDS Yet?!" etc. And he and his friends all laughed.

I don't think he came up with any of them; he was just a hateful parrot who hadn't yet graduated to edgier racist jokes. Like most Americans, he understood AIDS as a disease that infected only homosexuals and Ryan White, the apple-cheeked poster child for the "innocent victims" of the crisis, who contracted HIV from a blood transfusion when he was thirteen.

The bell rang, and we all quieted. Stevie's last fusillade rang out in the silence, a homophobic riff on the tagline for Trix cereal: "Silly faggot, dicks are for chicks!" Then he barked his signature manic laugh, a high-pitched parody of Woody the Woodpecker. "HahahaHAha, hahahaHAha, hahahahahahahaha."

Stevie and a handful of boys like him (it was always boys) were my primary education up until that point in what it meant to be gay. They taught me that my light blue sneakers were gay, that skipping was gay, and that if you looked at your nails by holding your fingers out instead of curling them in, *you* were definitely gay.

It was an odd but undeniable paradox of the time: Everything could *be gay*, but no one actually *was* gay. Not in my family, not in my classroom, not on sitcoms, not in books, not in the past or the present or the future. AIDS had put homosexuals on the news, but they were vectors for disease, not people. Occasionally, you'd hear a fag joke about San Francisco, but that might as well have been Oz. And in the absence of real queer people talking about real queer lives, boys like Stevie got to define our existence for us. I think Gen X queers placed such a high priority on visibility because we grew up in a black hole of representation. George Michael wasn't gay, and neither was Ellen, or Peewee Herman, or Doogie Howser, MD.

Just me.

And somehow, boys like Stevie all knew it. Or half-knew it. My sexual orientation was invisible, unclockable, and frankly a little confused, but my gender was a Lisa Frank Trapper Keeper: bright, weird, and obvious. Not feminine exactly, but not masculine, not boy, not straight, not *right*. And while some adults might pretend that gender and sexuality are unrelated—that being gay and being trans are entirely separate phenomena—children, bullies, and the Republican Party instinctively understand that the line between the two is porous and unimportant. I'd learned in elementary school to hold my tongue and never mention the inchoate feelings I had about other boys, but my body was ungovernable. When Stevie called me a faggot that day in class, it had nothing to do with whom I was fucking (no one) and everything to do with my limp little wrists that flapped like broken wings when I got excited.

"Stevie!" Señora snapped at him, and in that last instant before everything changed, I loved her more than I ever had.

We all waited for the hammer to drop, which in our small, suburban public school meant at worst being held for a day's detention. But Señora seemed unsure what to do once we were all staring at her. She had a high-key sensitivity for that oily, mocking tone children use to signal an insult, but she couldn't tell whom Stevie was making fun of. I wouldn't even look in her direction in case I somehow intimated I was the butt of the joke. After a long moment, she shrugged.

"Cómo se dice *faggot* en Español?" Señora asked, in that chipper voice she used to hype her fun lessons.

I'd heard adults use the word *faggot* before. I had both an older brother and access to my parents' cable, so films like *Blazing Saddles* and *Eddie Murphy: Delirious* entered my life very early. I liked the Dire Straits song "Money for Nothing" *because* they said *faggot*—or, more specifically, because they described what a faggot was: "See the little faggot with the earring and the makeup? Yeah buddy, that's his own hair." And I loved the comeuppance in the next lines: "That little faggot got his own jet airplane / That little faggot, he's a millionaire."

But this was different—official. Sanctioned. Like the pope when he spoke ex cathedra. We were in uncharted territory, and none of us knew if we were really supposed to answer her question (also I just don't think any of us knew how to say *faggot* in Spanish). Shock faded quickly to numbness, a sense that

I should have expected this. I wasn't angry at Señora, just disappointed in my own vulnerability.

"Pato!" Señora announced brightly. "Pero . . . "

She held up one cautionary finger, walked to the front of the class, and unscrolled the vinyl map of the world tucked at the top of every chalkboard. (Remember those? Old and rarely used, with an unpredictable number of Vietnams and Koreas.)

Spanish, Señora explained, was spoken in many places. Each had its own peculiarities, but we were learning textbook American Spanish, which would sound a little stilted to native speakers, so today she was going to teach us about Spanish slang. Words we knew already—like *pato*, which meant duck—had other connotations in other countries, and we had to be prepared for that.

For the next forty minutes, she pointed to different Spanish-speaking countries and explained their words for *faggot*—where I would be a *pato* versus a *mariposa* versus a *maricón*—with a bonus lesson at the end on *dyke*. I noted with a glazed and mild interest that *truck driver*, when combined with a female pronoun, meant lesbian—as did *crazy person*.

Years later, I'd discover for myself how easy it is to fail as a teacher, so I have some sympathy, but Jesus Christ, what the fuck was she thinking?

Sorry. I'm not sure why I'm writing this. Doing this is like channeling. When I open my mouth, dead selves come pouring out, each a poppet made from memory, using my tongue to repeat the only story it knows, the one it whispers constantly in the back of my head. Or maybe I'm just a cat with a hairball, horking up bits of myself I've never been able to digest. This isn't a thank-you letter or an accusation. I thought this might be an exorcism, but the ghosts haven't gone anywhere. They can't go anywhere. That's what makes them ghosts.

So call this a recognition: Señora taught me three critical things that day.

First, and most obviously: The nicest motherfuckers I knew could accidentally curb-stomp my heart at any moment. I don't think Señora disliked queer people, and if she'd known Stevie was making fun of someone specifically, I don't think she'd have taught that lesson.

I get it: This was 1990—homophobia was funny! And mean. And everywhere. There was not one out student or teacher in our town. We played a game called "smear the queer" at recess, a sort of reverse tag, where one person was the queer and everyone else tried to tackle him. Until the end of that year, the World Health Organization still categorized homosexuality as a mental illness, and US immigration law still saw being gay as a "psychopathic personality disorder" that was grounds for deportation. There were two high-profile antigay murders just in New York City that year alone (but also: until 2009, homo- and transphobic violence was not included in federal hate crime legislation, so who knows how many murders went unmarked). Señora was simply engaging with the world as it was, and as it was, the world was dangerous for me.

I wanted—want—to believe she didn't do this out of cruelty, but on some level, she felt this kind of hatred was trivial or acceptable, and without an apology, I can never forgive that. It's a small stone, but it's one that's been lodged in me since the seventh grade. Maybe I'm writing this so that if she ever reads it, she has to carry it too. For all I know, she already does. But that doesn't lessen the burden. Someone I trusted hurt me in a novel way, and that still hurts, no matter how many candles I light or jokes I crack.

And maybe, I've come to realize recently, I'm writing this because Stevie and all those other boys are still out there. Gen X went harder for Trump2024 than any other age group. But it's not just us. If there's one thing that growing up queer in the Nineties gave me, it's an antenna for danger, and it tells me that bad days are here, and worse are coming. A week ago on the subway, I heard one high school boy call four others *faggots* in the hateful-playful way I knew so well in the seventh grade. "You can't say that," the other boys gasped, and he yelled back, his face wide with joy, "It's 2025, FAGGOTS!"

And they laughed they laughed they all laughed.

Who am I kidding? My ghosts aren't even ghosts; they're cops, fathers, doctors, monsters, and sons. So maybe I'm writing this as a warning and a promise to the queer kids of today: We've made it through before.

The second thing Señora taught me? Propriety was never on a faggot's side. The rules of school (and of workplaces and adulthood) did not fully encompass me. This was . . . *interesting*, and while I mostly understood the negative side of it in that moment—that there were no protections I could depend upon—I would over the years find there was a second edge to this blade: The wall that doesn't protect you can't contain you either.

Third, and most importantly: *Faggots were everywhere.*

My understanding of queerness before that day in class went something like this: Queers were both a recent discovery *and* a biblical abomination, but most of them had already died of AIDS, so they also didn't exist.

That sounds ridiculous, I know. But we were the last analog children, the last American generation to make it to adulthood largely without cell phones or the practical internet. When you left your house, you became unreachable, and although sometimes all those empty hours felt like choking on air, as an adult now, I miss the luxury of that slack time. We were restless, and because the world could not yet shoot down our phone lines into our bedrooms, we roved out to meet it.

But if something wasn't printed on a piece of paper within a mile and a half of me, it might as well not have existed. We spent huge amounts of time trying to verify basic information. Debates over important issues like whether Bon Jovi sang, "It doesn't make a difference if we're naked or not," could last weeks, months, or forever if the damn lyrics weren't included in the liner notes. If I missed an episode of a favorite TV show, it was just gone—unless I was lucky enough to catch the whole season on a midsummer marathon, six months later, when no one wanted to talk about it anymore (there's a reason prestige television didn't appear until DVR was invented). When I was eighteen, I met a girl from Texas who grew up thinking Jewish people had horns, because she'd never met one and that's what a kid told her in Bible study. Ignorance was Gen X's normative state.

But each time Señora thwacked that map, she planted a bright pink pin in my understanding of the universe. There were lesbians in Colombia! Homosexuals in Spain! Here a faggot, there a faggot, everywhere a faggot faggot.

Years later, when I started studying queer history, I learned the name for this kind of unexpected revelation: *reading against the archive*, the practice of disentangling useful information from biased sources. But in the seventh grade, it felt like finding a clue to some grand mystery no one else was in on—a mystery where the stakes were my life.

In those analog years, my family had a computer, but it was mostly just a word processor, and it wouldn't even turn on without the right 5.25" floppy disk to provide its operating system. Out there somewhere, the World Wide Web was being spun, but those tendrils had yet to touch our town, and the changes they'd bring were inconceivable. So I knew of only one place to explore the questions burning inside me without talking to anyone or running into one of my classmates: the public library.

Our town library was a beautiful, dusty stone pile, smack-dab on Main Street, just a block from my house. It was built in the early 1900s by the children of robber barons, who paid Louis Comfort Tiffany to design its turtleback lamps and imposing reading room, but down the decades it had become less and less of a centerpiece for the town. The chandelier had been stolen at some point, and the hardwood floors had become so scuffed and scarred, it was just easier to hide them beneath thin industrial carpeting. There were no computers, just one old microfiche machine that was basically a glorified magnifying glass. But the giant wood doors still pivoted weightlessly on their hinges, so even a child alone could push them open easily. And once those doors drifted to a close, it was an exceptionally quiet place, the opposite of my home, where there were always six different people doing ten different things. I liked that I could hide there without hiding.

I didn't always like libraries, or words, or dream of being a writer and historian. And much as I liked Señora, Spanish was never my best class, even before all this. The idea that languages could function so differently was hard to wrap my head around. Why did Spanish divide the verb *to be* into *estar* (for temporary states of existence, like being hungry) and *ser* (for permanent states of existence, like being from New York)? I just couldn't grok it.

I don't blame Spanish specifically. Language always came in fits and starts for me. For the first four years of my life, I had only a handful of words, primarily *cookie?* and *NO!* My mother worked at a school for children with what were then termed "emotional disabilities"—largely kids we today would say were on the autism spectrum. She held her breath and let me develop, with the help of a veritable army of grandparents, aunts, and cousins to ensure I was almost never alone. Then, one day, I pointed to the saltines on top of our dented, harvest gold refrigerator and said, "I want a cracker." From that moment on, according to family lore, I spoke only in full sentences.

The same thing happened with reading. In the third grade I was in the lowest reading group, struggling with My First Readers. In the fourth, Mrs. Kiernan confiscated my cousin Emily's copy of *Interview with the Vampire* from me and told my parents I wasn't slow—just lazy. (She was, unfortunately, correct, and I hated her for it. Once she lost a book report I knew I'd written, so I waited until everyone was outside for recess and searched her desk until I found it. Surprisingly, this did not make her like me more.)

Since then, I had methodically devoured the entirety of the children's room at our library, from Judy Blume to *Redwall* to *The Great Brain* to my favorite, the diseased mind of Lois Duncan (who wrote both *Hotel for Dogs* and *I Know What You Did Last Summer*). Freed from the obligations of friendship, I burned through books like a chain-smoker, lighting one off the next. I could easily read three or four mass-market paperbacks in a week, an author's entire oeuvre in a month. After that day in Spanish class, I read faster than ever—largely because for a while I stopped doing homework, or anything else. It wasn't a conscious decision. I just stepped away.

That's what I thought of it as: going away. Away was a place inside me. It was easiest to get there while reading. I simply let the world of the book expand to fill my consciousness. But books weren't necessary. I could go away staring out a bus window or up at the asbestos ceiling tiles in health class. If acted upon, my body reacted—moved from classroom to classroom, answered direct questions—but it was otherwise largely uninhabited.

When I was away, everything was gray and OK. The world was a tepid place that held only mild interest for me. It was interesting to fail out of honors math. It was interesting to read Tamora Pierce's *Song of the Lioness* series over and over again, without understanding why the gender-confounding heroine captivated me. It was interesting to realize mid-read that I'd pissed my pants and would have to destroy my underwear to hide the evidence. Again. It was interesting to find the gun my father hid in the back of his closet, work out the combination lock, and hold its barrel to the side of my head. It was interesting to dig a hole in the backyard with my brother Johnny just to see how big a hole we could dig. Everything was equally interesting, by which, of course, I mean that nothing interested me, not for a second, and so I went away.

In the library I didn't need to go anywhere. There was no one to go away from. It was as gray and quiet as the deepest places inside me. I spent hours sitting in the rarely used nonfiction stacks, the dust itself seemingly frozen in the lengthening shafts of afternoon light, a decoy book perched on my knees in case someone spotted me.

Before, I'd done research for school; after that day in Spanish class, for the first time, I started researching for myself.

Using the card catalog was a little like doing a Tarot reading: I pulled a few mysterious cards, then tried to puzzle out their meaning. There were separate (but related) catalogs for authors, titles, and subjects—but the "catalogs" were actually long skinny drawers, filled with hundreds of index cards, hopefully in alphabetical order. Each card started life crisp and typed, but years of fingers flicking through left them stained, foxed, dog-eared, and illegible. Over time, a card might be updated haphazardly, in pen or pencil or by putting it awkwardly in a typewriter and adding the author's latest publication on a diagonal that obscured everything else on the card, like a fresh tag over a beautiful mural. Some cards offered you a mysterious side quest, just the words "see also" with no explanation of why or what you might also see there.

The card catalog was an obstacle course for nerds; Dungeons & Dragons for one; a slow dance with paper cuts and enlightenment.

Gay and *lesbian* got me nowhere. *Gay* had only been added to Library of Congress subject headings two years earlier in 1988, and until 1986, *The New York Times* had refused to print the words *gay* and *lesbian* at all. Vanishingly few books had queer protagonists, and most that did were published by small gay presses whose reach fell far short of our suburban shores. I wouldn't find a gay book written by a gay author in our library until Sarah Schulman's groundbreaking novel *Rat Bohemia* appeared seemingly out of nowhere on the new-fiction shelf in late 1995. If a mainstream book *did* have queer characters, it was considered impolite to mention them. In my senior year of high school, we managed to read Alice Walker's *The Color Purple* and most of Shakespeare's sonnets without ever once discussing queer desire.

But trying the subject card for *homosexual* got me a handful of nonfiction—all in art history. This confirmed one of my nascent understandings: Artists and homosexuals were somewhat interchangeable (and I ask you, where is the lie?).

I don't know what I hoped I'd find—some kind of *Tag! You're Gay* manual? But what I got were mid-century college art books. I don't know if anything is quite so disappointing as being a horny preteen and having to jerk off to grainy photos of Greco-Roman statuary. The statues were "homosexual" because the gods they depicted occasionally did drunken, depraved things—a 1950s understanding of Zeus was all 1990 had to offer.

And it was enough.

When I opened those books for the first time, a tremendous *crack* echoed through the silent library. The floors heaved up. The stacks caught fire. I began to see beneath the scrim of the world, what was hidden under what I was told.

THERE WERE GAY GODS.

Was that a vast oversimplification of thousands of years of sexual history? Yes. Did it save my life? Also yes.

Back to the card catalog I went. I had my work cut out for me: There were vastly more books coded "mythology" and "religion" than "homosexuality." Thankfully, the librarians were delighted to find a young person who understood the card catalog and Dewey decimal system and soon hired me to work as a page. It was my first job that wasn't babysitting or catching the crickets that infested my neighbor's basement. In retrospect, there was no small amount of pity involved in taking on the loner who slammed the card catalog shut any time someone approached. Did the librarians need me? Probably not. But they knew I needed them.

Adult books on mythology turned out to be boring, but they soon led me to fantasy and sci-fi—an unloved section of the library, full of cheap paperbacks with onionskin pages that turned translucent on contact with my oily adolescent sweat. I read the most derivative shit ever published, knockoffs that might as well have been titled *Lard of the Rings* and *Star Truck*. My vocabulary lurched in a pseudo-medieval direction, studded with squires, palanquins, and diadems, preparing me for the SATs and life as a jester at the Renaissance Festival.

Many, if not most, of these books were heterosexual fantasias, where women were the reward for being a good person (/man). I learned how to write thin, stereotypical characters by watching Robert Heinlein recycle the same bimbo scientist/sidekick in book after book. There was the occasional effeminate male villain or female love interest whose theoretical bisexuality was a sign of her enlightenment (and a titillation for her strapping man-hero). But just like in the real world, I couldn't find actual gay people.

Months passed in the quiet stacks, with only Señora's voice in my head: *pato, mariposa, maricón*. We were out there somewhere, I knew it.

Eventually, through sheer brute force, I found what I was looking for in the pages of a skinny fantasy novel called *Magic's Pawn*. On its cover, a sadboy with wild hair cuddled a horse with distressingly human eyes; inside, a lonely gay boy found himself and, eventually, love (and a psychic horse too). Vanyel was bookish, friendless, and terrible at sword practice (aka medieval gym class). It took sixty-nine pages for him to turn down a licentious tavern wench and think, *Why am I so different*, and thirty more before he learned the slang for gay in his world: "Shay'a'chern."

Despite everything I've forgotten, I still remember that.

I read every volume in the series, and then everything the author, Mercedes Lackey, had written. These were not gentle YA novels; they were filled with rape, child abuse, and revenge killings. They showed a dangerous world where Vanyel rarely had the chance to stop fighting and simply exist as a happy homosexual with a psychic horse.

In other words, they might as well have been nonfiction.

What future did the real world offer queer kids like me? Silence, disease, and death. A 1989 study by the US Department of Health and Human Services found that 30 percent of youth suicides were queer kids; around that time, 20 to 40 percent of homeless youth were estimated to be queer, and around 75 percent of AIDS deaths were queer men. At least Vanyel had a horse.

Soon I found other, weirder books, where sex, sexuality, and gender were nothing like the limited options we had in the Nineties. Sure, they were always set in space, or another dimension, or the far future. I didn't believe the visions they showed me were possible, not in any tangible way. But they liberated my imagination, accidentally giving me the thing I needed most: hope.

For a long time I was jealous of the kids who came just a few years after me—the ones to the internet born; the digital natives who were never alone, not in the way we were. They carried the world in their pockets. But now I see what a weight that is and how excruciatingly free I was when there was nothing to plug into. I would never say we had it better, but I will say this: Compromises were made; there were trade-offs, losses. This book is my attempt at a balance sheet; a record of what we got for what we gave; a recognition on a personal and generational scale.

No magic horse ever found me, and I didn't make any new friends until high school. But that day in Señora's class set me on the course I've been running ever since. Unknowingly, she dropped a key, and it turned out to be the one I needed to unlock my future.

So maybe, in some ways, she's still one of my favorite teachers. Or at least, she had the most effect on me, and I'm pretty happy with who I am these days. And turns out, it's sometimes hard to draw the line between "because of" and "in spite of." I used to think I was a goldfish, grown to fit the container I'd been born into, but I recently learned that goldfish will grow again if given a new home, so either I have to keep evolving (exhausting, perhaps inevitable) or give up that metaphor (it's cliché anyway).

Maybe I'm just still trying to grasp the difference between *ser* and *estar*, between permanent and temporary, between *who I am* and *who I just happen to be for now.* But to put these stories on the page, I've got to pick a verb, a tense, a self.

Honestly? I'm not sure I want to tell these stories, but it turns out I can't tell any others until I get these out, and that means putting it all into language, even the contradictions. Maybe the contradictions—the moments where I least fit the old world I was born into—matter most of all.

So Señora, if you ever read this: Thank you. And fuck you. And goodbye.

Beyond the Pale

FRIDAY NIGHT IN MY HOMETOWN IN 1994 WAS AS QUIET AS any other night, unless there was a girls' basketball game, the one sport where we seemed capable of producing winners, in which case the volunteer fire truck might zoom up Main Street, with several players in our school green ("Lady Bulldogs," as they were unfortunately known) hanging off the side as it passed the eight alphabetical streets that made up the center of town: Astor, Buckhout, Cottonet, Dutcher, Ecker, Ferris, Grinnel, and Home Place. My father and I knew it was unlikely that anything would be open: 9 p.m. in Irvington might as well have been midnight on the moon. But we had a job to do.

Zarelli's (our preferred deli) was long closed, as was This 'n' That and the pizzeria, but Squazzo's light was still on, and even though he was obviously cleaning up, the door dinged open when we pushed. We shopped like domesticated zombies, wandering up and down the single aisle, grabbing whatever penetrated our shell shock: a bag of Doritos, a gallon of milk, a stack of sundry Entenmann's baked goods. When we got to the counter, I asked for cold cuts—a pound each of whatever he had.

"Machine's off," Squazzo grunted, swinging his big head toward the slicer behind him as he tallied and bagged our things. "Having a party?"

"My grandmother's dying," I said, the only thought in my mind, the response I'd have given if he'd asked my favorite color or who won World War II.

For the length of a blink, we stood silently, considering the small hole I'd torn in the social fabric.

"A pound of each," he nodded, turning the slicer back on.

In seventy-two hours, my grandmother's obituary would announce that she was "survived by six daughters, a sister, thirty grandchildren, and twenty-one great-grandchildren."

As of 11 a.m. that morning, they were all headed to our house, an old Victorian that had been torn down, expanded, and rebuilt until there were windows on the outside without a corollary on the inside; a four-floor warren that could, when necessary, house an army (or whichever members of our family were currently most in need). My grandmother had survived colonization, revolution, immigration, the Great Depression, the British, the Americans, World War I, World War II, *and* her own father. Where she was going now, she could only go alone, but until that last moment, we'd be with her.

My grandmother smelled of holy water and Oil of Olay, the two vials always on her dresser. She wore clip-on ersatz pearl earrings, and when she wasn't around, I clipped them on myself—sometimes on my ears, but just as often on my nose or the meat of my arm. Sometimes she'd chase me around the house with a pair of scissors threatening to cut my tongue out, and I'd run giggling to hide in the clawfoot tub we shared (everyone else used the downstairs shower). She had an old fox stole that I thought was the most glamorous thing, and so I draped our adopted alley cat, Tarzan, around my neck when I wanted to look fancy. She listened to AM talk radio 24/7, so I did too. I still remember the commercials for Tiger Balm, garlique extract, and shark cartilage pills; how excited I got for Paul Harvey to tell me *the rest of the story*.

Two years before she died, I introduced my grandmother to "electronic mail" via Prodigy, our first internet service, which randomly generated a string of numbers as your email address. I knew a handful of other people with computers at home, but we were the first to go online (in fact, according to the World Bank, in 1992, only about 2 percent of Americans used the internet). We gathered around the gray behemoth of an IBM, and as we listened to the modem sing its static song, I explained that we could contact anyone, anywhere. A portal to the entire world, with no long-distance charges or peak pricing hours, right there in our partially finished, wood-paneled basement.

"Josie?" My grandmother asked—her last living sister, the one who stayed behind.

No, I explained. Anyone who *also* had an email address. But then I realized we didn't know anyone who had email yet, so my grandmother gamely pronounced the whole business "nice," and my parents helped her back up the stairs. I felt the past walking away from me, as I stayed behind, seduced by the screen. I didn't know yet what the internet could offer, but I understood it was a door, and I was desperate for a way out.

When my parents dropped me off at Cornell for my freshman year in 1996, the last thing we did was set up my computer. I heard the heavy dorm door click closed as I plugged wires into ports, and when I looked up, my father—terrified—stood in front of the door my mother had just exited.

"Your mother says I have to talk to you about sex," he said to the tile floor. He had a gray newsboy cap in his hands, which he absentmindedly twisted like a dishcloth. He was a bookish Catholic straight guy from Washington Heights, born in 1944, so technically, he wasn't even a Boomer—he was part of the aptly named "Silent Generation." He used to joke that our family motto was "suffer in silence." It would have been a hard conversation even if I'd been straight. Instead, it was impossible.

After a long pause, he nodded slowly to himself.

"There. Now I can say we talked."

My grandma and I shared a room from when I was five until I was fourteen, the same one she died in. When I was in middle school, she once caught me staring at the old man whose bedroom window looked in on ours.

"What are you doing?" she asked, in a tone that said she knew exactly what I was doing.

"Nothing," I shrugged, and we never talked about it again.

But a few months later, I went to turn off the TV at the end of the evening (we watched Channel 5 news every night from 10:00 to 10:25, when the sports came on, then said our prayers and went to bed), but I accidentally spun the knob to Channel 13, our PBS affiliate. Rosalind Russell appeared on screen in a bright orange kimono waving an elegant cigarette holder. I moved to turn it off.

"Wait!" My grandmother's voice stilled my hand, and my introduction to camp—in the form of the classic film *Auntie Mame*—began. We watched Russell swan around some fabulous party, Connie Gilchrist trailing behind her, playing the role that was my grandmother's life: the thick-brogued Irish maid, always at the party, never on the guest list.

(My mother was furious when the local paper headlined grandma's obituary "Alice Twomey: Cooked for Babe Ruth." But grandma said Babe was pretty nice. He'd taken pity on her, a new colleen in New York City, fresh off the boat in 1926. Not a lot of jobs for girls who left school in the fifth grade, but she knew how to cook and clean, and there were rich people everywhere. He gave her tickets to the World Series, but she didn't know what that was, and who had time to go to the theater anyway, so she threw them out.)

We watched the campy adventures of Patrick Dennis and his auntie Mame until well past midnight. It was the latest we ever stayed up, the only time I remember her insisting I watch something. She bought me the book for Christmas that year.

Looking back, I think she was trying to give me something she knew I needed but did not herself have. Community. Context. An idea of a life outside our room.

After a long silence, my father turned to my mother.

It was an anonymous weeknight in 1996, the spring of my senior year of high school; it was a moment I'd been imagining for a decade. Still, I bungled it. I tried again and again all evening long, but the words refused to leave my throat, until it was nearly midnight, and I raced into their bedroom like a crazy person and mumble-shouted, "I'm bisexual!"

"He didn't get this from my side of the family," my father finally responded, flummoxed. My mother put down the mystery novel she'd been reading. "We'll talk about this in the morning," she said, her eyes focused on a distant nowhere.

I slinked back to the basement and logged on. "I did it," I typed to my virtual friends. "I told them."

One of the open secrets of the early internet was just how damn gay it was. By 1996, the year I entered college, somewhere around 20 percent of all AOL users were queer. Not that they wanted us there: In 1998, AOL outed a closeted servicemember to the US Navy, which got him dishonorably discharged, but he fought in court and was allowed to "retire honorably" instead. There was no such thing as a safe space, but there were degrees of danger, and you didn't need to be a computer scientist to know that. The options we had before were bad; the internet was new. And so an entire generation embraced it with the kind of hope that is indistinguishable from desperation.

Maybe, just maybe, we'd find something better on the other side.

After her father tried to kill her, my grandma fled Ballyconnell for Canada. She spent two weeks in steerage on the SS *Megantic,* but she paid her own way. It took a while, but eventually she joined her sisters in Norwood, the area of the Bronx once known as "Little Belfast," where my mother and her sisters would be born.

Once, grandma told me, one of her sisters left the Bronx for Sunset Park, a similarly Irish neighborhood, but in Brooklyn—the far end of the civilized universe. "No one will ever visit you," grandma told her. And no one did. Not out of spite; it was simply too far. She had gone beyond the pale.

One year later, she moved back.

Grandma and I did everything together. We went to church several times a week, where I'd fall asleep on the kneeling benches that ran under the pews. She taught me how to make crepes and how to check that the butcher hadn't hidden old, gray ground beef under a layer of fresh pink.

In the fourth grade, we had to interview older relatives. I used a heavy, plastic Fisher Price cassette recorder with oversized buttons for fat-fingered children. It's the only time I remember her talking about her childhood, how the kids in her village celebrated St. Stephen's Day by finding the body of a wren and building a bier to bear it around town, asking for donations for its funeral, which they then used to have a bonfire in the woods. She taught me a song to ask for pennies for the wren, which I can't remember. Neither of us could sing for shit.

I didn't ask her what it felt like to leave behind everything you'd ever known for a slim chance at a better future. But the day was coming when we'd have that in common too.

I chose Cornell for many reasons. Secretly, a big part of me thought I wouldn't get in and I could put off college for another year to figure some things out. And if I did get in, it was massive, some 20,000 undergrads. I'd been trying to find real live gay people since the seventh grade; just playing the odds, there had to be a few in that sea of students.

Plus, my parents wouldn't let me look at schools more than five hours away from home. Cornell was five and a half, which was nowhere near far enough for me and far too far for them, but I knew they wouldn't argue about it. Education was the key to a better life; they'd always told my brothers and me to get into the best colleges we could, and they'd find a way to pay for it. My parents were of the first generation on either side of my family to go to college and here I was headed to the Ivy League. My life was becoming unimaginable to them. They understood survival as a communal activity, and all I wanted was to run.

Much later, I found out that grandma's father, my great-grandfather, was known as "Terrible Terry." He survived the many famines wrought on Ireland by British colonization and fathered thirteen children (most of whom survived to adulthood). All it cost him was his soul.

After grandma died, her sister Josie told us there was a song about Terry's terrible fists in the local villages near Cavan, but she'd never tell us the lyrics, hoping instead to let the violent past die quietly with her. Every year or two, I fruitlessly scour the internet for a whisper of a tune about a man I never knew, who made choices I will never face or comprehend, for whom love, death, family, and freedom were intrinsically interlocked.

That part, at least, I have over the years come to understand.

The funny thing is, I *did* get it from my dad's side of the family: His sister was a low-key butch who kept her hair cropped tight and wore pants and a button-down shirt every day. But she was born paralyzed on one side of her body, and never moved away from her mother, and sang beautifully in the church choir, so no one ever thought of her as a sexual being. She taught me to shake hands "like a man, not a limp fish." This was a gift. She would have done anything for me, but all she had to offer were instructions for building a better closet. (We never talked about being queer, but after she died, I found her college girlfriend, who confirmed what my baby gay heart had long suspected.)

I *also* got it from my mom's side of the family (if there is any argument for a genetic component to sexuality, it's my family tree). My cousins Tara and Pat owned homes with their "friends," who came to all the family events and stood close enough to touch without ever once touching.

During a party—Christmas, or maybe Easter?—I walked in on my mother and my aunts discussing whether Pat was gay.

"I'm going to ask him," my mother said, flustered by something I hadn't heard. "I'm just going to ask!"

"If he wanted you to know, he'd tell you." The words leaped from my throat, but to this day it still doesn't feel like *I* said them. "Leave him alone."

I walked right back out of the kitchen, unable to stop myself, afraid I'd already said too much.

I wasn't consciously waiting for my grandmother to die before I came out, but every time I imagined it, I was older—in college, usually—and she was never around.

Like most Irish of her generation, my grandmother never learned Gaelic; the British had banned it centuries before, which is perhaps why so few American words come from it, despite the massive Irish American diaspora grandma was part of. The words that did make the jump sound so Irish, you feel it as soon as you hear them: *galore*, *colleen*, *shebeen*, *fiacre*, *phony*.

The phrase *beyond the pale*, to mean something unimaginable or unacceptable, may also come from Ireland, though not the Irish. "The pale" was the part of Ireland under British rule in the late medieval ages, which was originally demarcated by fence posts (or "pales"). The walls were as much to keep the Brits *in* as the Micks *out*—they were sick of their colonial countrymen falling in love with "natives."

The morning after I came out, I left the house before dawn—technically, I think, my first time sneaking out, though it was only to go to school without having to talk to my parents. But they were waiting when I got home. They must have taken the day off work, it occurs to me as I write this. They were panicked.

My cousin—my mother's closest kin, who was also my high school guidance counselor—was with them in the kitchen when I walked in. My mother had called a few of her sisters (which ones, I wondered idly, slipping deeper inside myself as they talked around me). They all agreed I should see a therapist and shouldn't tell anyone else. Was I sure? Did I even know what I was saying?

Like that, my secret was gone; other people telling other people the thing I had told almost no one for years. And yet somehow I remained trapped inside it. At school, too, someone told someone who told everyone, or maybe just three people, but either way, I could feel eyes on me all the time, and all I wanted was to disappear.

(The therapist was alright. He didn't try to "cure" me or anything, which was pretty cool, considering that conversion therapy on minors was legal in New York until 2019. I don't think my parents even wanted to change me, though if I'd spontaneously woken up straight, they'd have been relieved. Though I didn't realize it at the time, they were just as confused as I was. They had no models for being the parents of a queer child. I was furious at them, so I approached therapy like a game I was determined to win. Every answer I gave ended with "but my parents": but my parents were upset; but my parents were sad; but my parents were angry. When they came to pick me up from that first session, the therapist told them I was fine, but he thought *they* might want to meet with him. We never discussed therapy again.)

What have I added, and what have I subtracted?

These memories are faded and well-worn, pajamas I slip on when I'm alone. I mostly remember remembering them. The interview tape is long gone. We never talk about my coming out, all of us happy to let those bad years grow hazy. I still don't know who told my brothers. The historian in me recognizes these memories are as much Shroud of Turin as Rosetta Stone.

Grandma first started getting sick—really sick, dangerously sick—around the same time my older brother Johnny went off to college, so I moved downstairs into his room in the basement, which had been our cousin Christian's room before him and would be my brother Jim's room after me, and then eventually my aunt Eileen (Christian's mother) moved down there, and then our cousin Kathy bought the house, and . . .

Our place was a decades-long game of musical chairs.

Pubescent (and with a room to myself for the first time), I used our dial-up modem (which literally *called the internet* over the telephone) to find Usenet bulletin boards, which were a sort of precursor to Reddit: threaded comments filled with weirdos and porn. In places like soc.motss (society—members of the same sex) or alt.homosexual, you could download a single pornographic jpg in just a few hours. You were never quite sure what you were going to get, and about half the time the file was corrupted, or your connection failed mid-download, but still, it felt like unfettered access to the libido of the world (at least until someone else needed the phone). Like most kids today, the first gay sex I saw was digital, and the first people I came out to were strings of text and blinking cursors.

I had no idea that these spaces were coming of age right along with me. Usenet was invented in 1979, the year after I was born. Soc.motss came along in '83. The first official Usenet group for queer youth wouldn't be created until 1994, two years after I went online, and by the time I found it, I thought it was boring. Official, asexual, and rulebound. The opposite of what I wanted from the internet—but still, a sign that we were out there in growing numbers (even if I never once met another queer person my age online in those years).

I spent my midnight hours in mIRC chat rooms, where I was entirely untraceable—you chose your name anew each night, and in that anonymity I found honesty. The people I was talking to didn't matter. They had no way to hurt me, and if they reacted badly—or even just took too long to respond—I logged out. And if they responded well? I logged out anyway. Not once did I stay in touch with someone I met in those rooms. That would have defeated the purpose. It was easier to say *what* I was when no one knew *who* I was. Growing up in a big family in a small town, I'd literally never had that experience before.

And it turned out, on the other side of loneliness was freedom.

Spontaneous advice I did not want from relatives: Join the priesthood; get a girl pregnant; stop throwing it in our faces.

The priesthood? When I was nine, or maybe twelve, our parish priest gave a sermon about people leaving Mass early after getting Communion. "If you love God," he said, "an hour a week is nothing." *He's right*, I realized, sitting on the kneeling bench below the pew, staring at my grandmother's simple, black Mary Janes. *I must not love God.*

Church was boring and implausible and soaked in hypocrisy, though I loved the incense, the vestments, and the pomp.

Once I moved down to the basement, I discovered that the house was a giant refracting device, easily carrying the sound of a cough or a creak multiple floors down to my bed, creating an auditory map that allowed me to live like a ghost, entering only just-emptied rooms, drifting out before anyone returned.

All spring and summer of my senior year, my parents and I fought mostly in silence, my preferred weapon. I could disappear with the best of them. On the worst nights, I slept at friends' houses or occasionally, if the weather was nice, in a broad, flat-limbed tree in the park down Main Street. It wasn't so much anything we said as it was the feeling of vulnerability I hated, that I never knew when I woke up who would be there or what they would know about me.

I didn't tell anyone what was happening, even the few friends I'd come out to in real life, because what were they going to do? Lots of people knew that my friend Patty's dad was a shit-kicking drunk who took everything out on his daughters, and no one (kids or adults) did anything about that. Your family was your safety net was your prison, and if you got a bad one—sucked to be you. My parents were kind, always wanted the best for me, were paying for me to go to college, and would never have hit me. I was nearly eighteen. It was time to shut the fuck up and take life like a man, not a limp fish.

Suffer in silence: I knew how to do that. I meditated my way through the days like a monk on fire.

When she was four, grandma told my tape recorder, she had scarlet fever. They had no money for a doctor; at that point, her father was sharecropping for a local landowner, who paid him a potato a day. She was delirious with fever, fading, starving. He saved her half of his daily ration, a futile gesture for a dying daughter.

But she lived.

When partition soon came to Ireland, Ballyconnell became a border town, tucked just inside the Republic. When we visited in the early Nineties, our relatives thought it was good *craic* to give us directions down a cow path that ended in machine guns and barbed wire.

Like all borders, the line between the North and the Republic was inked in blood. For years, armed raids and guerrilla reprisals swept through Ballyconnell like seasons. Once, my grandmother, her father, and an older brother hid in a ditch while British mercenaries burned nearby farms. When her brother passed out, my grandmother took his rifle. She was twelve, probably, or perhaps fourteen (though I remember her saying she was nine, that date doesn't match my research, so who knows). Whenever I hear the word *terrorist*, I see her face.

The Black and Tans went a different direction that day, and again, she lived.

And then, when she was seventeen, she let a Protestant boy walk her home from a village dance, and my great-grandfather tried to kill her himself.

"It's the lonely life," my mother said. "Is that really what you want? To be alone?"

And I did. At least a little, for a while, to see who I was or could be when I wasn't with them. That's what really scared them, I realize now, not just the gay stuff.

As my parents were about to drive away, leaving me to face freshman orientation and the rest of my life, my mother leaned out the window and grabbed me in an almost painful hug. "Don't join any gangs," she whispered urgently, barely able to get the words out. "You're already in one."

She was right about that, though I didn't feel it at the time. But the great gift of my family is that I have always known what a loving community looks like—even if sometimes it felt like I was observing it from a doorway, unsure whether I belonged in that embrace.

This was a fundamental question of the queer Nineties: Did being gay automatically make you an outsider? We thought *maybe—maybe*—but we hoped *maybe not*. Only the years to come could tell.

My grandmother passed beyond the veil around 3 a.m. on Sunday morning, May 8, 1994—almost exactly two years before I came out to my parents. We were all there with her, as my aunt Kathleen—a hospice nurse—gave her the final dose of morphine. I was holding her hand when she took those last strange breaths, so different from the endless number of unmarked ones that preceded them. A rattle, a gasp, a silence.

And then she was gone.

I wonder if they were all waiting for her. Her sisters. Her father. I wonder what happens to all the rage and sadness once you make it to the other side, or if there is another side.

I wonder if she's waiting for me. There's so much I never told her.

Solve for Mass

I WENT TO PROM BY LUCKY ACCIDENT. IN MY SENIOR year, I was asked to join a study group in physics. These were the popular kids in my grade, and it felt good they wanted me around. We'd been in school together since kindergarten, but it was as though we were meeting for the first time at seventeen and discovering that—tentatively—we found each other agreeable. There were five of them: two couples and Tanya, whom I'd been friends with in the first grade but hadn't really spoken with since. For weeks our study sessions had been filled with prom planning, and Tanya was increasingly frantic about being the single one who messed up their perfectly symmetrical plans. Finally, one afternoon as we prepped for midterms, she asked if I knew anyone who didn't have a date for prom.

"I don't," I admitted, trying very hard to let it lay there neutrally. I wanted to go, but I didn't want her to know I wanted to go (in case I didn't end up going), and I certainly didn't want her to know I was hoping she'd ask me. That kind of public wanting was my least favorite emotion; it felt pathetic, and I knew other kids could sense it the way dogs smell fear.

Tanya pretended to jot down something about force or acceleration, but I could feel her staring at me from the corner of her eye. "Do you . . . *want* to go?"

"Sure—" I started to say, but she cut me off to clarify, " . . . as friends!"

I'd come out to a handful of other students in the previous two years, but my first and only high school hookup was a straight jerk who outed me to a bunch of people, so by this point, I kind of assumed everyone knew.

"Yeah, right, friends," I nodded, and she looked relieved.

I was basically a mannequin needed to balance seating arrangements, which was perfect. They had been planning for months, or maybe since birth, and I got to ride the coattails of that work. I saw it as preparing me for a lifetime of attending hetero formalities as a kind of embedded cultural anthropologist, eager to try their rituals and judge them harshly. Like weddings and team sports, in the Nineties, prom was part of the straight world I planned to leave as soon as I could.

But it turned out? Prom was awesome.

Armed with those disposable plastic cameras that were given out at every celebratory event back then, we were ready to have a full twenty-four exposures of fun. Around midnight, we ended up at a "teens' night" at Club Exit, a Manhattan megaclub over on the far west side of 56th Street. Ever since the Paradise Garage opened in 1977, the desolate West Side of Manhattan, from Soho to Midtown, had all the best places to dance. Larry Levan, the DJ at the Gay-rage (as it was colloquially known), basically invented the modern club experience—made for dancing, with the DJ at the center. Along with his friend Frankie Knuckles, he got his start spinning at the Continental Baths, the same NYC gay sex club that launched the careers of Bette Midler and Barry Manilow. I didn't know any of this until years later, when I curated a show from Levan's archive, but I loved the styles they created: Levan invented garage music (aka the New Jersey sound), and Knuckles (who DJ'd at The Warehouse in Chicago) invented house. I was one of countless queer kids whose bodies they put in motion over the decades.

There must have been a million people, maybe two, at Club Exit when we arrived, and we were revealed, in our rented finery and googling eyes, as the suburban mice we were. Our crew posted up by a column, determined to soak up every moment on our allotted schedule of Cool Things (even the ones we didn't particularly enjoy). We stood in a circle and affirmed that we could not, of course, dance in the tuxes and dresses we'd have to return the next day. That was why, of course, we weren't dancing.

Of course.

But I was a night owl in those days, comfortable in my skin only when everyone else was asleep, and in those dark hours, local radio was my constant companion. Specifically, I listened to the endless beat of 103.5 KTU—"Keep It Turned Up!"—the local dance station. *Another night another dream but always you . . . from the back to the middle and around again, I'm gonna be there till the end, 100% pure love . . . pump up the jam, pump it up . . .*

It seemed I knew every word, every beat, and every break breaking over the revelers on every floor of that club. (*Of course I did*; it was a basic teens' night, made for basic bitches like me, whose understanding of house music came from *Jock Jams, Volume 1*, but I didn't know that then and I felt so cool.)

Like Kevin Kline in *In & Out*, I could not resist the beat. I was a pimply, effete, 110-pound nerd with badly lopsided hair—what could I possibly do that would embarrass myself more than simply existing? Plus, everyone I knew at the club was extravagantly drunk. And if they remembered anything, *fuck it*, school was over in a matter of months anyway.

I slipped my jacket off and handed it to Gerard; wiggled out of my shirt and tossed it to Ben; and then I was in the crowd wearing just a sweat-slicked undershirt.

On the dance floor, the rules of physics we'd been studying came to vivid life: The lights moved like liquid, the beat from the speakers physically pumped my heart, and I was both a photon and a wave; a person and a piece of something bigger; I was alone, and I wasn't lonely at all.

I don't think we stayed more than thirty minutes after that; we still had to get to Jones Beach to watch the sunrise, then back to the suburbs for a hungover breakfast as we all sang "Fast Car" at the top of our lungs. But however long I was on the dance floor, it was enough time to reach euphoria, that embodied state of joy where your brain is dethroned, taking both the past and future with it, leaving you in the eternal, animal present. I've found it other places—communal religious rituals, orgies, good tabs of ecstasy—but nowhere as reliably as the dance floor at 2 a.m. It is the feeling of being at one, of a purpose; an invocation of the social nonself; the place where I first understood all the meanings of "mass" simultaneously.

It's the best feeling I've ever known.

By the time I got to college, I was eager to explore this newfound vessel, my body. Gym classes—dance classes, specifically—were a low-key way to do it. Again, I knew no one, so how could I be embarrassed? Plus, Cornell understood it was a school of nerds, so the policies around physical education were forgiving: You had to pass two semesters, but if you failed, the classes were deleted entirely from your transcript. By spring of my freshman year, I understood this meant I could sign up for as many as I liked, take them for four or six weeks until the workload in my other classes became overwhelming, then simply melt away. I failed modern dance, belly dancing, African dance (twice), swing dancing (two, maybe three times), contact improv movement classes, tae kwon do, massage—no, massage I passed, because I was hung up on my massage partner and his girlfriend—ultimate frisbee (another crush), etc.

To be honest, I enjoyed being bad at dance class—it meant there was never a moment where I had to think about being good, or successful, or "where this was going." My parents were strivers who'd wrestled their way out of the working class, and in my suburban high school, everything was a competition. I thought being bad at something meant you were a failure, but when the only measuring stick was how much fun I was having, "bad" lost all meaning.

I never got better at memorizing steps. But I learned how to join seamlessly with the crowd: how to give and receive energy, how to wordlessly ask and express consent, how to mold my body to the rhythm of someone else or be the solid base they wrapped themselves around, and, most of all, how to look sexy while I did it.

(Later, my partners would tell me they have a word for this in the theater, folks who are *movers* but not dancers).

The classes were fun, but they didn't have the transformative power I'd found at Club Exit on prom night. The lights were too bright, the lines were too clear, and we were all *learning*, that kind of future-focused activity that tethers your mind inescapably to reality. There was a small dance floor at our local gay bar, which was fun, but they only played about fourteen minutes of decent music each night, and they closed at 1 a.m. Our queer student dances were held in the same hall where the student government met, giving them all the sensual ambiance of a model UN meeting. And in both cases, I knew everyone in the room, making it hard to let go, which was what I was really looking for: oblivion.

To find my way back to that nothingness I experienced post prom, I retraced my steps. All throughout later high school, friends and I would head into Manhattan now and again, looking for some measure of coolness we could absorb by osmosis (since we certainly never talked to anyone). But we were day-trippers, returning at the latest on an 11 p.m. train; the night city was not for us. It was purely a logistical issue, you see: From 11:30 p.m. to 6 a.m., there were no trains to our town, and we'd all been told if you didn't flat book it from

Times Square to Grand Central after the last bow at *Les Mis*, you'd be eaten by homeless junkies.

It had only recently occurred to me to ask, What if the junkies were hot?

At the end of the millennium, in New York City, queer life hid behind the thinnest of curtains. It was still a world largely safe from the perversions of heterosexuality; I don't remember ever seeing a straight celebration—be it bachelorette or birthday party—at a gay bar. But that world wasn't hard to find. All you had to do was cross the line into certain neighborhoods, and it enveloped you. Eighth Avenue from Chelsea to the West Village thronged with queer spaces, from sex shops to bars to cafés to therapists to tacky club-wear warehouses. Straight people were allowed, of course, but they weren't particularly welcome. One day soon the curtain would be torn down, and queer people would come flooding out into mainstream life. But what we gained in reach, we lost in density; I'm glad it's not all we have, but I miss those glitter ghettos of the '90s. They had all the problems of the rest of the world—racism, misogyny, childhood trauma turned into weaponized therapy speak, capitalism—but with one critical difference: They were built to serve people of different backgrounds.

Queerness is a fickle blessing. Unlike religion, ethnicity, class, or race, it's rarely shared between parents and children or neighbor with neighbor. So queer people don't often grow up experiencing gatherings of people *like us*, and when we create those gatherings as adults, they're more likely to be diverse along other lines, out of simple necessity. This has never stopped a White queer person from being a racist asshole (for instance), but it does mean we've got slightly more chances to get off that train if we were born on it.

In 1996, a little before I came out to my parents, I tried to go to the youth group at the LGBT Center in Manhattan. I'd found a calendar for the center on one of the Usenet boards I frequented, written up in ASCII characters, and that made me aware of the group's existence. But I chickened out blocks away every time, not frightened so much as overwhelmed; I knew I wasn't living my real life, but I couldn't commit to stepping through that door and announcing who I was just yet. Instead, I lingered on the doorstep, in a place called The Big Cup.

The Big Cup was like a gay bar's younger, nonbinary sibling: a queer coffeehouse for teenagers, people who came out so late they felt like teenagers all over again, and chickenhawks. It had a kind of Delia's catalog, girly, mid-'90s/retro-'60s aesthetic: mismatched couches surrounded by deep pink walls with large, casually drawn chartreuse flowers stippled randomly around the room. The staff was a queer version of a Benetton billboard: every race and gender of hot.

I spent a lot of time in the Cup dreaming about meet-cutes that never happened, though I got bolder over the years: Once I gave a guy behind the counter my number (he froze like a rabbit in the shadow of a hawk, and we never spoke about it afterward, even years later, when I occasionally worked as a go-go boy at a monthly party he threw at a dyke bar in Brooklyn). Queer kids had no dating examples to follow, and most of us had spent our lives perfecting fake emotions. To put the real ones on display, in public? Eventually I could imagine doing that at The Big Cup, because I literally never saw a straight person there. But in the regular world? That wasn't going to happen.

As I started exploring the city by myself during college, the Cup became my usual first stop, because no matter what day or time it was, there were always promoters hanging out on the sidewalk, passing out party flyers or copies of the free gay weeklies *HX* and *Next*. These mags were a microcosm of NYC queer culture. They profiled D-list gay celebrities (some of whom, like RuPaul, would go on to real fame), promoted all the parties that week, and had ads for adult massages, gay tax professionals, and viaticals (vulturous companies that preyed on people with AIDS by buying the rights to their life insurance payouts). At the back of each issue was always a montage of photos, usually a three-to-one ratio of naked-people-in-clubs to men-in-suits-at-AIDS-fundraisers. With God as my witness, I swore that one day, it would be my bare navel pixelated on that back page.

It was in these magazines that I first got a sense of the wide world of queer aesthetics, the million ways one could look like a fag or a dyke if your life didn't depend on mainstream success. The last of the infamous Club Kids became my style icons as I became femmier and faggier every day.

Oh, those ecstatic children! I can still picture them, in their wild outfits that took weeks to put together and faces that took hours to paint. They branded themselves as perverse fun personified, taking names like Julie Jewels and Mistress Formika, and went on daytime talk shows as proud queer freaks demanding to be seen. They were a gasp of fresh air in a stultifying decade.

Via the weeklies and the party flyers that littered Eighth Avenue every Monday morning, I learned the landscape of Manhattan's queer nightlife, slowly separating the venues (Twilo, Limelight, Roxy, Tunnel, Escuelita, Splash) from the parties (Kurfew, Jackie 60, Click 'n' Drag, Papi Chulo, Motherfucker, Meat). On weekends, nights generally started at 10 p.m. and went to 4 a.m., and if you arrived before 11, entry was free or greatly reduced.

Starting my sophomore year of college, I'd frequently take the last train into the city, walk to a club, get in for free, stay until they closed, walk to Grand Central, and take a sunrise nap inside until the trains started running again. If I was feeling flush, I'd rent a locker in Grand Central for the weekend (this was before 9/11, when it was easy to find places to leave your luggage), so I could go out Friday night, change Saturday morning in the bathroom, nap wherever, hit The Big Cup, go out again Saturday night, then take a Sunday morning train to Westchester or a bus to Cornell. My aesthetic was candy raver light: I'd wear giant JNCO jeans with metallic crop tops, a thousand jelly bracelets, Rocket Dog platform sneakers, "freedom rings" (rainbow necklaces that were briefly *de rigeur* in queer spaces), and a cancer-causing amount of body glitter. It seemed like everyone in the clubs but me was smoking, so I'd bring a new outfit in a big Ziploc bag in my pocket, and when I left, I'd seal away my now sweaty clothes to keep the stink from permeating my homework. There was nothing I could do about my hair, though, which was long and thick and absorbed the humid club air, swaddling me in the funk of a thousand homosexuals for days afterward.

My favorite club was Tunnel, 80,000 square feet of dance floors, DJ booths, and go-go cages in an old railroad terminal. There was a ball pit, the scuzziest indoor fountain you can imagine, and a Kenny Scharf–designed room covered entirely in fake fur (FAKE FUR! In a club. Back when people smoked indoors. What the actual fuck?). Twilo had better sound, Cafeteria had better DJs, and Limelight was just sexier—plus I loved that they had a separate entrance for straight people, who only got to experience half the club. But Tunnel was more *fun*, a place still filled with outlandish Club Kids even after the OG demon twink Michael Alig murdered his lover Andre Melendez in 1996 and the scene unraveled.

That world was disappearing even as I first touched it, I understand now. And it wasn't just because Alig had become the infamous "party monster." The wild, hedonistic, fuck-you energy of those demented dolls was a response to the death march of AIDS all around us, and the introduction of retrovirals in '96—the first actually effective treatment to control HIV—transformed their world as surely as it did every other part of queer life. Suddenly, the future was available to them again, and with all that time stretching before them, it was just less interesting to dedicate your entire life to preparing for Friday night.

But it was damn fun while it lasted.

The line outside Tunnel stretched from 27th Street on down to Twelfth Avenue some nights, where it touched the remains of the West Side Highway, the long-abandoned roadway where trans liberation activist Sylvia Rivera lived in a tent community of unhoused people. The highway was basically a gritty parking lot that would soon be gentrified and renamed Hudson River Park. But back then, it made going to Tunnel feel dangerous and far from the businessman core of Midtown Manhattan. Thankfully, over my years of going out, I got to know folks who worked there—Mary the Door Whore, Flashlight Kenny, DJ Superboy, Maxx Headroom—and more often than not, they'd pluck me from the line and let me in. Some mornings, as the sun peeked over the horizon, I'd stick around as they all got cashed out, and we'd head down to Chinatown for dim sum brunch or, if we were lazy, to the all-night diner that was right around the corner, Moon-something? It's long gone now, like the club itself, probably condos. They noticed me *because* I was a solo weirdo, night after night, and they recognized in me a fellow traveler for whom nightlife meant something more than a chance to get sloshed under good lighting. In the club or on the web, we were all looking for places to try our new selves on and to see those selves reflected in the massively dilated pupils of our peers.

One night (must have been around 3 a.m., because all the performances were done and the place was thinning out), I ran into a drag queen in the bathroom. We were at a party called Kurfew, which was for young queer folks, largely ex-suburbanites like us. The music was an endless blur of house, happy hardcore, and hip-hop and pop remixes, but I had terrible taste, so that was fine by me. I'm sure parts of it were sketchy: I got offered drugs regularly, and once I had to punch a guy in a k-hole to get him to stop lazily grabbing my dick on the dance floor. I was already deep in my sober sister years by that point. Until I was thirty-two, I actively avoided anything that might have loosened my tongue, and that protected me from many of the dangers of nightlife. But Kurfew was also a cheesy, sweet, weird-teen world with an online message board where kids gave each other advice on how to come out. In my earliest clubbing years, Kurfew was my home base.

The queen was my age, studying something at NYU, and from Long Island; her look was trapped awkwardly between Jewish mother and Liza Minelli (note: she was not a comedy queen); I can't remember any of her names, birth, chosen, or stage. She was trying to hide that she was crying over some stupid boy who only liked her in drag; I was trying to hide that I didn't have a lot of money, so when I got thirsty, I drank water from the bathroom faucet.

Thinking I was puking at the sink, she kindly pulled my hair back.

"All natural," she whistled in appreciation. She petted my long hair and took in my look, my massive silver lamé pants that seemed like a skirt when I stood still, my glitter eye shadow and sweat-streaked mascara. "Guuurl!" she drawled. This happened a lot when I was out in those years: People aggressively used gendered terms (sometimes kindly, sometimes cruelly) in an attempt to figure out what I was.

"Sort of!" I shrugged, not realizing she'd think I was talking about my hair, not my gender.

"I use clips too." She laughed, pulled a fake chonk out of her hair, and clipped it to mine. Then her knees buckled, and she slid to the ground, still holding my hair, so down I went with her.

Her real problem, she explained drunkenly, was not that he only wanted to fuck her in drag. It was that she didn't mind that he only wanted to fuck her in drag. And what did that make her? She'd never thought of herself as a trannie (it was the '90s, cut us some terminological slack), but she liked herself better in drag—and people liked her better that way too. Not just men. Out of drag, she was Boyname Whatshisface NYU-Student the Third. In drag she was—well, I can't remember, but she said it with fireworks, and it lit up the bathroom.

She loved herself in drag, and she wouldn't mind being a woman, and frankly, she thought it might make dating easier. Was that . . . *enough*? Was it OK for her to start 'moning?

I had no answers, though I had recently begun to consider similar questions. I knew of "transsexuals" only that they were rare and sad and had an overwhelming sense of themselves as the "opposite sex" from the moment of birth. If you didn't fit that model, then you were just a faggot with flair. But if sexuality existed on a spectrum, could gender?

This was a realer conversation about queerness than I'd had in any of my classes at Cornell, even the women's studies ones, which were fascinating but more concerned with theory than reality. It was these small interactions with other gender weirdos—interactions that almost exclusively happened in queer spaces—that first helped me feel OK with my own confusions and contradictions. If enough people had these kinds of questions, maybe it was alright that none of us had any answers. At least, that's what I told her over waffle fries at the diner. We never saw each other again, and I wonder if that night made any impression, or if I was just one of the randos who bounced off her, the way so many bounced off me in those years. It was the mass that mattered, not any one moment.

Most nights, though, I went to and left the clubs on my own. Hooking up was integral to the lure of going out but rarely part of the actual experience for me, and even when it was, I preferred to leave it on the dance floor (or in the bathroom stall) when the night ended. Cinderella had the right idea: show up, look fly, leave them chasing after you. As for going out with friends—at first, that's what I thought I wanted. A crew, a context, a group like a spaceship, from within which I could safely experience the world. Unfortunately, I discovered that years of spending most of my time on my own had made me a little fascist; I was easily annoyed when friends wanted to leave early or get wasted, or just generally harshed my mellow.

There were—*are*—times when this makes me feel like a bad person. To be alone is to be a failure. To want to be alone? That's sociopathic. It's selfish, antisocial, and the very thing my mother worried about: the lonely life. And the more time you spend alone, the more you all but guarantee that the moment will come when you *want* people around, and there's no one there for you. As a childless homosexual, I worry about being lonely and old and abandoned to the ravages of capitalism. But the older I got, the more I found there were some things I just preferred to do by myself. Dancing was chief among them.

No, that's not quite right. There are no independent organisms on the dance floor, just one being with a thousand heads: the mass. And it was easier to join when I wasn't leashed to three other people with their own agendas for the night. I wanted hours where nothing existed outside the beat in my ears, the sweat on my skin, and the multitudinous exchanges of energy with strangers, who were simultaneously a part of me and I of them. It bridged the poles I was pulled between, my need for solitude *and* community.

Eventually Tunnel was shuttered by Mayor Rudy Giuliani, part of his all-out war on nightclubs in New York City, but nobody really noticed because three weeks later was 9/11. The West Side was soon redeveloped as a playground for the rich. The queer parties got smaller, weirder, and more underground. But they never stopped, never will stop, can't be stopped. Dancing is sex on a communal level: an embodied ecstatic ritual of union. It is a fundamental human experience, even if these days I mostly do it in the kitchen with my partners and our cats.

When I needed it, the dance floor broke me down in the best way. I've never known a runner's high, but thirty minutes at a rave left me feeling euphoria long before I discovered ecstasy. I learned to love my body there—not what it looked like, that was a longer journey—but the meat of me, the muscle.

My body is a bag of blood with some floating organ islands; it is a temple, a playground, a spaceship. Everything I am is my body, even my brain, which still likes to believe it's better than all the rest of this (now) forty-seven-year-old flesh—more knowing, more in charge. But when my heart beats faster, my brain pulses with it, and when the music pulls me to the dance floor, it eradicates all the lines between you and me, and me and me, until only the mass of us is left, alone and never lonely.

Frankenstein and the Monster

My first college coming out happened a week into freshman orientation at Cornell. As I waited in line for the dining hall's bottomless pasta station, a girl with the biblically unfortunate name of Salomé told me that her friend Rumeli—whom I had never met—had a crush on me. My instinct was to smile, make some small noise of appreciation, and quickly switch lanes to the waffle bar. But Salomé was a top high school athlete, and I, a potato of the couch variety, and she herded me like a hungry velociraptor until I was trapped with my back against the conveyor belt of the dish return.

Salomé interpreted my evasions as adorable shyness, which kicked her predatory matchmaking instincts into high gear. She would arrange everything: the time, the place, the eventual wedding. All I had to do was say yes.

Most important moments in my life I can only spot retrospectively, once there is a further story for them to provide the origin to. But in this moment time seemed to freeze, and I could feel all my potential futures fractaling outward. *All I had to do was say yes*, and the machine would kick into gear; though they might fit uncomfortably and eventually strangle my soul, the trappings of heterosexuality would accumulate on me with ease, like plastic bags in the limbs of a dead tree. Or I could dissemble, say something that meant nothing, and take on the double life I'd sensed in my closeted teachers and relatives. Or I could—

"Salomé, I'm gay."

—let the chips fall.

Salomé's face in that moment—pop-eyed, slack-jawed, bright red—looked like Elmer Fudd after that wascally wabbit socked him a good one. She choked and stumbled away; I got a bowl of meat tortellini with meat sauce.

Months later, Salomé found me in our dorm lounge, tenderly took my hand, and asked if I felt homosexuality was a personality flaw I could overcome; in an act of poetic revenge, my friend Danni plastered the commons with cutouts from hardcore gay porn rags she'd found in a bus depot. Every night for a week she put them up, and every morning for a week the RAs tore them down, and after that Salomé avoided our floor.

(Rumeli turned out to be quite nice.)

Salomé's reaction was extreme mostly because she didn't hide it, but the shock undergirding it was not uncommon in my undergrad experience. Cornell often felt small-*c* conservative: sheltered, suburban, fratty. My first semester, I met only three other out queer freshman—and I was actively looking. The student body was big enough that you could find a little bit of anything, but it was like picking glitter out of a bowl of milk. Without social media, our intel depended on the rumor mill or—if you were lucky—the buttons on someone's backpack, which proclaimed their allegiance to the Dave Matthews Band, Free Tibet, or those Budweiser frogs that said, "Wazzzzup."

On an essential level, I had told Salomé the truth: I had no interest in dating Rumeli because I had come to college as much for the sodomy as the degree. If sexuality was a multiple-choice test, I was going to tick that gay box hard.

But on a more practical level—on the level of boners, wet dreams, and the persistent animal of the body as it exists before and beyond language—my sexuality was a messy essay, full of contradictory assertions and little primary evidence. I spent a lot of time trying to divide my feelings into "real" and "unreal." Attractions to men were real. How could they be anything else, if eighteen years of entrenched heterosexual training had done nothing to diminish them? Attractions to women though . . . they were suspect. Less likely to happen at first sight, easier to ignore, more common when I was younger. Were they lingering holdovers from a lifetime of heterosexual conditioning? Stress dreams? Erectional accidents?

America had discovered bisexuals just the year before, when *Newsweek* ran its 1995 cover story "Bisexuality: Not Gay. Not Straight. A New Sexual Identity Emerges." That sounds ridiculous, I know, but even up through the mid-1960s, *bisexual* was often used as a scientific term to mean intersex. In the Seventies, some rock stars came out as bisexual—Elton John,

David Bowie—but they all later picked a side, with Bowie infamously telling *Rolling Stone* in '83 that saying he was bisexual was "the biggest mistake" he had ever made, and he was really just a "closeted heterosexual." Elton John, for his part, married a woman in '84, then came out as gay in '88. Freddie Mercury, in response to a question about his long-rumored bisexuality, said, "It's a thing schoolboys go through. I've had my share of schoolboy pranks. I'm not going to elaborate further." Prince repeatedly told reporters he was "not gay" but refused to say anything else. Eventually everyone just agreed to forget. It was the Seventies after all—people did too many drugs, had too much sex, and believed in crystal healing. The whole decade got a dirty pass: They were druggie sluts, but they weren't *really* bisexual. No one was, anymore, in the '80s—except maybe Madonna, who said everyone was somewhat bisexual, but also that she didn't believe in labels. But her whole schtick was to be sexually shocking, so no one thought it was anything more than an attempt to grab some new headlines. With every celebrity who came out as bisexual, bisexuality seemed less real.

The *Newsweek* story did a complicated dance, declaring bisexuality was real while also invoking all the fake and temporary tropes that were used to argue that it wasn't. It also made bisexuality seem menacing and fun: "Bisexuality lurks as a rupture in the social structure, conjuring fears of promiscuity, secret lives and instability."

I mean . . . *sign me up!*

But I had a problem. It was commonly understood there were two kinds of bisexuals: bisexual men, who were really gay; and bisexual women, who only existed for four years (or however long it took them to finish college). The mid-Nineties had a veritable cottage industry of films squatting on the monosexual edges of bisexuality: *Threesome*, *Three of Hearts*, *Chasing Amy*, *The Pillow Book*. Saying you were bisexual was generally seen as a soft launch for coming out as gay. Qualifying as a "real" bisexual seemed like a math problem: Prove that your attractions (as measured by emotional weight, duration, and penetration) are equally divided between men and women, or fail.

If the world really was divided that neatly between gay, straight, and fifty-fifty bisexual, how could I be so confused?

I felt often in those years that I was somehow fooling myself. When it came down to it, I seemed to have two kinds of sexual feelings: ones that developed immediately upon seeing someone (men, usually androgynous ones), and ones that developed either from getting to know someone or because the situation itself was erotic (which could happen with anyone). Yet the one thing everyone seemed to agree on was that sexual orientation was the first-order question, the dividing line, the determiner of who you *could* be attracted to. Everyone had one (a singular sexual orientation, that is), and they didn't change or shift or operate differently at different times, *except* if you came out later in life, in which case you were granted a sexual mulligan, and everything that happened before was immediately discounted.

Alfred Kinsey had declared in the late 1940s that sexuality existed on a spectrum, but even that was interpreted as a rigid dictum: If you were a Kinsey four, you were a Kinsey four at all times and for life. This inflexibility was fundamental to the idea of queer identity at the time. From a gay perspective, this was a way of pushing back against conversion therapy and the idea that being gay was "a phase." From a straight perspective, if sexuality was changeable, who knew when the trap door might open beneath you and drop you into gay hell?

My orientation seemed gay, but my desires seemed bisexual, and every once in a while the wires crossed entirely, and my body responded to a woman the way I normally responded to men. Since the Nineties said none of that was possible, I was either unreal or wrong.

(It was a relief to come across Pat Califia's book *Public Sex* toward the end of my time in college. Although Califia later came out as a trans man, Califia at that time identified as a butch lesbian and wrote about preferring BDSM with cis gay leathermen over vanilla sex with women. It was the first time I heard someone acknowledge what seemed true in my bones: that sexual orientation was real but also limited. Unfortunately, *Public Sex* was not on the recommended freshman reading list.)

Instead of wrestling with those contradictions, I dodged my way through college, coming out as gay or bisexual, whichever seemed more likely to get me what I wanted in the moment. Eventually, once I got over its slurry connotations, I embraced *queer*, whose indeterminacy was a blessing that got at the heart of the matter: I was—and I was interested in people who were—*not straight*. I almost never had crushes on straight people, of any gender, and when I did, learning they were straight usually killed it. With men, what was the point of lusting after someone I was never going to hook up with? And if I did hook up with them, they were almost certainly going to be bad at it, and then afterward, what if they made me discuss sports, or worse, Pearl Jam? Whenever I had sex with straight guys, they imprinted on me like chaotic ducklings: Some wanted to be guided to the lake of homosexuality; others pecked me out of the room any time they saw me thereafter. I quickly developed a rule: You had to be *this gay* to ride this ride. I was confused enough myself; I didn't want to be someone else's training wheels.

With women, it was the opposite: I was anxious, timid, and only ended up following through if they made the first move. It took years to fully acknowledge, let alone enjoy, anything tainted by straight culture. Most of the women I was attracted to were butches or cougars anyway, so at Cornell it was rarely an issue.

What did it mean that I was predominantly attracted to people who looked queer? Diddly *and* squat. We had no concept of a sexual identity that wasn't determined solely by binary sexual object choice. I was just a weirdo attracted to other weirdos.

To explore all these questions, I engaged in what I later learned was a time-honored, foundational queer experience: cruising tea rooms.

(If, at this moment, you are picturing kettles, macarons, and British matrons, brace yourself.)

Cornell had a huge and bucolic campus, with libraries and class buildings and dorms spread across 700 rolling acres, which meant there was a veritable smorgasbord of glory holes to choose from, conveniently located in or near whatever building your punishing class schedule revolved around. They were always in the unused bits of busy places: the basement, or the top floor, or that weird little hallway that led nowhere. The most active one was right in the heart of campus, in Goldwin Smith Hall, which was open all night, required no ID to enter, and had so many bathrooms that the inconvenient basement one with the cranky heater was pretty much only used for getting head.

Cornell, like all prestigious and pretentious institutions, had a policy of doing whatever was required to keep students from getting arrested, so they mostly turned a blind eye to our shenanigans. But they knew, and everyone knew they knew, because once a month the insides of the stall walls in that bathroom—and *only* that bathroom—were painted black in an effort to cover up the ballpoint personal ads: *I suck midnight Thursday* and *fck here 2 a.m.*

Students, faculty, visitors, staff—you never knew whose foot might be tapping on the other side of the stall. Cruising sidestepped all the messiness of labels and self-awareness and emotions. It was exciting, frightening, and endlessly new; each night a different adventure for the brave of heart and big of dick. Sometimes five guys jerked off furiously in a circle, like a hot summer squall, in and out in five minutes, every surface sopping wet. Sometimes it was just two of us, and we'd go to the top floor, find an unlocked seminar room, and fuck on the wide, uncomfortable wooden tables.

Cruising was a dangerous pastime, and most other cruising grounds I encountered in those years were frightening: truck stop bathrooms and abandoned wooded paths. No one told you where to go, but if you kept your eyes open, you could find the traces: condom wrappers on trails, holes between bathroom stalls, and (always) horny and desperate graffiti. Cornell's manicured lawns and all-night studyfests made cruising there seem like a safe option for men from miles around. It still had the thrill of the forbidden, but you were fairly certain you could get help if someone turned violent. And in those days before electronic keycards and constant surveillance, campus buildings were easy to get in and out of. The number of out queer students at Cornell in 1996 was very small, but the supply of guys who wanted something they could only get at a urinal at three in the morning was inexhaustible.

We never talked during these furtive moments. I was too ashamed, too afraid, and too disgusted to admit that I liked the intense and strange pocket universes we created in those rooms. They were places of few words but easy communication; an entire sonata of desire could be revealed in the rhythmic sideways glances of the person standing next to you, cock flopped in the palm of his hand, stiffening with each flick of his gaze.

But the moment I exited those rooms, everything became complicated again. I had sex dreams about a close female friend, often found myself attracted to people whose genders I couldn't tell at a distance. I was great at the hands-on parts of being gay; it was the hypotheticals that left me spinning, the impossible truths my body was telling me: that desire and gender were often related, but not always, not for me; that sexual orientation was real but not necessarily the permanent dividing line of my attractions; and that it was far more interesting to see what my body *could* find erotic than to presume what it *couldn't*. I was reinvestigating the entire field of sexology, one orifice at a time.

Thrumming underneath all of this, though, was something harder for me to think about: my gender. Or maybe my sex? I'd never felt much like a boy, never picked the boy toys, rarely had boy friends—yada, yada, yada. But I didn't feel like a girl either, so it was easy to see these feelings as isolated failures that didn't add up to any kind of bigger meaning. Besides, in the Nineties, any sign of gender weirdness was mostly seen as an indicator that you were gay. Boy George? Gay. Sylvester? Gay. Pete Burns? So fucking gay. If a TV show wanted to have a character that everyone knew was gay but didn't want to say it openly, they just made them feminine. Queer gender and queer sexuality were rarely discussed, and in the mainstream, that discussion was always through and for ignorant straight people, so the categories of our existence all seemed to collapse in on each other like a faggy black hole.

But as puberty took the wheel in high school, these amorphous inclinations gained new urgency. My body was changing: thickening, growing hair, lopping off the last reedy squeaks of my once-high voice. I disliked it—the hair on my legs, the weight in my gut. I couldn't put it into words, but I missed my indeterminacy, the way my gender had often been inscrutable when I was younger—a point of embarrassment if someone commented on it in front of my schoolmates or brothers, but which otherwise brought me a strange surge of pleasure.

Could queer be a gender?

With no idea of what I was doing, I began to stumble toward those feelings—those moments when the animal of my body purred.

I started by growing my hair. This was around 1994, and I could have pretended to be emulating a plethora of long-haired men: Kurt Cobain, Jordan Catalano, all thirty-seven members of Rusted Root. But talking about what I was doing (or worse, why I was doing it) was impossible. So one morning, I simply stopped parting my hair on the right (the way our local barber, Sal, styled my dad and older brother and me every month) and instead parted it in the middle . . . and then didn't touch it again for two years. For the rest of high school, my hair was extravagantly lopsided, a prank I pulled on myself. Every morning I hoped I'd wake up with long Leonardo DiCaprio locks framing delicate features and high cheekbones, but instead my mirror showed a frizzy-haired refugee from *Dilbert*.

Slowly I settled into a mid-Nineties neo-hippie/baby-raver style that made great camouflage for the queerly gendered. I slit the legs of my pants and sewed in panels to make them voluminous, skirt-like bell bottoms. I encrusted myself with acceptably masculine jewelry, which at the time included pendant necklaces on simple leather straps, ear cuffs, toe rings, eyebrow rings, bandanas, and bracelets with stick figures of Kokopelli woven on them. I wasn't trying to look like a woman, but I was trying very hard not to look like a man.

Why? I couldn't say. I'd seen *The Crying Game*, and while I was fascinated by Jaye, I didn't think I was the same thing she was. I felt closer to the incoherent identities of the leads in *To Wong Foo, Thanks for Everything! Julie Newmar.*

Early on in the film, if you haven't seen it, Wesley Snipes concisely explains the American understanding of gender in 1995: "When a straight man puts on a dress and gets his sexual kicks, he is a transvestite. When a man is a woman trapped in a man's body and has a little operation, he is a transsexual. When a gay man has WAY too much fashion sense for one gender, he is a drag queen."

Putatively, Snipes et al. are drag queens, but throughout the film, they never wear male clothing, and at the end, when a woman says, "I love you Ms. Vida Boheme," Patrick Swayze replies, "I've waited my whole life to hear those words said to that name."

I knew I wasn't the first two things, so maybe I was the third? If that was an option, an acceptable way to be gay in the Nineties, that seemed alright to me.

That was not, however, an acceptable option. Though everyone loved *To Wong Foo*, in the real world, those queens would have had their asses kicked from one end of America to the other.

It's hard to remember exactly when the violence started, but by the end of my freshman year at Cornell, my gender had begun to shine like a reverse Bat-Signal, calling the assholes to me. Most of them were run-of-the-mill chickenshit homophobes, anxious to proclaim their heterosexuality by calling me a faggot or a he-she under their breath when they passed or throwing a half-finished Snapple at me from their car. It was *always* Snapple. The bottles were made of heavy glass that exploded violently when they hit the sidewalk; they must have been fun to throw.

Then there were the guys whose skin I really got under. The pair that spontaneously slammed me to the ground when I was walking around New Haven, Connecticut, one night, then kicked me halfheartedly and walked away. The trust fund kid who stalked me around Cornell, pinning me against the wall of my dorm once to tell me a mix of *what he wanted to do to me* and what it looked like when his hunting dogs tore foxes apart.

Shit like that could go down anywhere, any time. In April of '98, a bunch of us from Cornell went to Princeton for the "Second Ivy League Lesbian, Gay, Bisexual, Transgendered [*sic*] and Allied Conference," which was mostly unmemorable. On Saturday night, they held a party, at which the same seventy-five people who'd been at the conference stood around chatting and mostly not dancing, until around midnight, when there was a sudden influx of drunken party boys. A handsome butch blond in khakis ("church pants," as I thought of them) pursued me through the dim smoky rooms, throwing his arm around my waist and hauling me bodily onto the dance floor. Guys my age were always so tentative in public, this was an exciting shock, even if he wasn't my type. We danced close together for a song, his hands firmly cupping my ass and pulling me into him, and then he bent in to kiss me. We made out for a minute, until he paused, pulled back, squinted at my face, and kissed me again.

This time he stopped almost immediately and pulled away—though he kept one hand on my ass. With the other, he patted the soft downy hairs on my cheeks and said, "Dude . . . are you a dude or a chick?"

Absolute, drunken confusion washed over his face as I told him I was, indeed, a "dude." He staggered back, threw up on the ground in front of me, and stumbled out of the party, drunk and horrified. Some part of me felt like I had won a skirmish in an invisible war, and some other part of me cried and cried and cried, and I could reconcile those emotions no more than I could my gender itself. The next day, the conference organizers told us they had been some group of straight assholes, a frat or a team or something, who'd come to fix the lezzies and frighten the fags.

That feeling I had in seventh-grade Spanish—that I was outside the bounds of propriety, always potentially vulnerable, a deer in open season—hardened into a certainty.

It's hard to convey the extent of the violence queer people faced in the Nineties, a conversation that has faded into academic debates about whether or not Matthew Shepherd was killed because he was gay. But his was just one name among many: Tyra Hunter, left to die in the road when the EMTs who responded to her car accident realized she was trans. Brian Mock and Hattie Mae Combs, burned alive by neo-Nazis. Barry Winchell, the army sailor whose body was pulverized because he had a transgender girlfriend. Brandon Teena, raped and killed for being a trans man. Julio Rivera. Billy Jack Gaither. Scott Amedure—murdered after he appeared on a "very special" episode of *The Jenny Jones Show* to confess his crush on the man who killed him three days later. The Last Call Killer in New York. The AIDS Commission killings in Minneapolis. The bombing of the Otherside Lounge.

And those were just the murders, the ones that were known. Most of the violence was routine, unreported, unpunished, like those frat boys at Cornell who set fire to a wooden statue outside our dorm while yelling, "Faggots"—an incident considered so minor I can't even find a student newspaper report about it.

Out queer people walked around with the whine of a missile in our ears, always wondering if it was about to land on us.

Our salvation was, of course, each other. The flipside to the violence was the community. Once I passed that visual threshold—once I could be read as queer at an easy distance—long-haired, flat-chested, in a knee-length crushed-velvet coat with nail polish that did not match my complexion or stubble one bit—I also crossed through what I can only describe as a door to the multiverse. There was an entire parallel plane of queer existence. It was small, yes, and by this point it had been battered by AIDS for nearly two decades, but it wove through the straight world like gold thread in an otherwise drab fabric.

I first became aware of it one Friday afternoon in the spring of 1997, when a butch grad student gave me the "dyke nod" as she passed—a quick jerk of the chin, which could mean "Hi," or "I got your tab," or "Get your hands off my girlfriend." We'd never met, but through the gay rumor mill, I knew vaguely that she was a vet student. "Need a ride tonight?" she asked. Ithaca had one gay bar, The Common Ground, which had moved to a desolate area outside town years before, after its original location was firebombed. On-campus options for queer fun at Cornell were few: There were weekly discussion groups called Men Supporting Men and Cornellesbians, but both had a sad tinge to them. They felt like AA meetings in hidden rooms with bad overhead lighting and uncomfortable chairs. There was a once-a-year gay dance, but mostly we had CGs. To get there on a Friday—when the gays and theys of a dozen upstate colleges packed their student night—you had to know someone with a car. Over my six years in Ithaca, I traveled in the packed back seats of more strangers than I could count, people who looked out for me simply because we were rainbows in a grayscale world.

Some version of this happened everywhere I went: A cashier in a bus depot in Utah complimented my two-inch platform sneakers and gave me a free ticket for the Greyhound; a waiter in New York City comped my meal and told me to check out a queer club called The Tunnel; and an endless number of closeted students sidled up to me in class, wanting to sit next to me or study with me or just pour out their souls for seven intense and never repeated minutes. I could show up in any small city in America, and by that evening someone would tell me what bar or café or house party to go to. It was magical. Far from being the lonely life, being out when I was in college felt like being in a secret society.

We *always* find each other.

By the late Nineties, I had also begun to find language for myself—largely on the internet at first and mostly adjectives: *androgynous, bio-boi, genderqueer, transgendered*. None of them fit comfortably though. I switched my major to women's studies and read all the queer history I could find. But even there, the line between gender and sexuality, trannie and faggot, seemed confused and confusing.

Gay New York was the ur-text of the field in the Nineties, an incredibly important work that defined queer history for decades to come. Yet, when it covered Jennie June, who described herself in her early-twentieth-century autobiography as "a woman whom Nature has disguised as a man," *Gay New York* referred to her as a "homosexual" who had taken a woman's name to "[mark] his transition from the straight world to the gay."

This was the state of gender in the 1990s: Trans people were acknowledged to exist, but they were extremely rare and only counted if they had, or wanted to have, "the surgery." (For years I thought there was a singular surgery, some kind of nose-to-tail procedure like a compound complex equation, adding, subtracting, multiplying; turning Y into X.) "Transsexualism" had only entered the DSM (the guidebook for psychiatric disorders) as its own entry separate from homosexuality in 1980. There was no idea of "nonbinary." Androgyny was a style—not an identity you could inhabit. Even most queer people saw gender as something of a conveyor belt, a constant motion toward an expected end goal of cis-seeming male or female. My mincing steps toward femininity made sense in that schema, but the longer I stopped in the middle, the more the ground disappeared beneath me. Shit or get off the pot—that was being trans in the Nineties.

Of course, trans people existed then, and they gathered in the disreputable places where they could: working-class bars, community magazines that you could only get via the mail in brown paper wrappings, and the hinterlands of the internet. But even in those spaces, they were still hashing out who they were—who we were? The first book I remember reading by a trans person about trans people was Leslie Feinberg's *Transgender Warriors*, a towering work of independent queer scholarship published in 1996. But the original subtitle of the book was "From Joan of Arc to RuPaul," because "transgender" wasn't an identity—it was an umbrella term for a collection of gender-crossing behaviors, which is why places like Princeton still used "transgendered."

These days, there's a rush to dismiss the increase in bi and trans identification among Gen Z as poser behavior, virtue signaling, and social contagion, as though who and what we were in the '90s was somehow the perfect distribution of queer identities. But today's young people are the first to grow up with ready access to these ideas, so of course they know themselves differently—better, I suspect, then we did at their age.

I thought for a while about starting hormones—not legally, of course; I'd ask a lesbian friend about getting a birth control prescription I could take. It felt like the necessary next step, what I *had to do* if I was trans. But it also felt like it would take me just as far away from where I wanted to be as I was now, just on the other side of some line that felt increasingly arbitrary. What if I wasn't moving *toward* something I wanted, just *away* from something I didn't want? Was that . . . allowed? Who could give me permission, I wondered, to be myself?

If in college I could have flipped a switch and woken up a cis woman, I'd have done it. I wanted, more than anything, to have kids, and it seemed far easier to do that as a woman than a gay man. Barring that, however, what I wanted seemed yet again unreal: gender à la carte. Facial and body hair? No. Breasts? No. Muscles? No. Genitals? I could go either way, didn't matter much to me. Clothes? Female. Pronouns? Neither/either. (I considered *ze* for a minute, I really did. It didn't sound real, even to me.) Could I have pieces that didn't add up to a whole, and could I swap them out for other pieces later on? Could I be Frankenstein *and* the monster?

No. No, the answer was no: There was no ground there.

Even in Cornell's queer spaces I often felt like a mutant—and it was worse in straight places, where I wasn't just weird, I was a threat. I was *just trying to provoke people*, as an aunt told me at Thanksgiving when she saw my painted nails. Provoke them into what, I wondered. Did they think I wanted to be treated like shit or just that it was my fault when it happened? The more I tried to listen to what my body was saying, the less I seemed intelligible to anyone else.

But something funny happens when you spend too long in freefall: You start to wonder if you're actually flying. I could stare in the mirror telling myself I wasn't really there for hours, but no matter what I said, there I was, staring back. I existed, even if I didn't make sense, and aside from the hours when someone (often, me) was telling me there was something wrong with me, I was happy. So a few years into my gender journey, I stopped trying for something specific and tried just letting myself *be*.

I only ever admitted my trans-ness to one person in college, and that only once, and in silence. My friend Ari and I met my junior year and soon became thick as thieves, stylish queer badasses who planned protests and orgies and conferences together. Ari's mother had had a girlfriend back when he was a kid; he used to joke that he came out as a dyke for the first time when he was five, trying to emulate them. By the time we met, he'd gone through puberty, still thought of himself as a girl, and was trying to parse it all out: Perhaps he was bisexual?

Or maybe he was right the first time, and he was a dyke? Or maybe he was asexual? We talked about sexuality all the time, but it wasn't until I was about to graduate that I remember us saying anything about our genders.

We were standing in a circle with two other people in a hallway in his dorm, loopy with exhaustion because we had just put on a three-day queer conference with hundreds of attendees. For some reason, we were doing a silly icebreaker, the kind where you step forward or raise your hand to claim various identities. When he said he felt trans—not was, *felt*, I remember that—I raised my hand as well. He looked at me quizzically, but before either of us said anything, one of the other people made a joke about how balanced our little circle was: two men, two women, two straight people, two gay people. I felt an intense relief as the moment passed, and we never brought it up again. I was surprised when years after we graduated, he transitioned. I shouldn't have been. By that point, so many of our friends had begun to shake loose the bounds of gender. In retrospect, I discovered, I'd had a whole world of trans and enby friends around me the entire time, each of us wrestling quietly with our own impossibility. Each building our own monster.

Me? Just a few years after leaving Cornell, I had the great fortune to get a job working with a community of young queer kids, many of them involved in New York City's ballroom scene, for whom the mutability of gender and sexuality was just an assumed truth. In their reflection I saw myself more tenderly and accepted that the rangy animal of my gender was going to do what it wanted, even if it didn't make sense to me or anyone else.

For a while, I thought my students were just somehow intrinsically more liberated, but now I'm pretty sure it was the consequences of growing up in a postinternet society. When I stumbled onto the World Wide Web as a freshman in high school in 1992, I was part of an entire generation downloading a new operating system for reality. Is it any wonder that the film that became our symbol of the digital future—1999's *The Matrix*—was created by two closeted trans women? Online, new nameless groups of queer people were able to find one another: gender weirdos, asexuals, folks whose desires seemed to change over time or respond to stimuli other than bodily sex. Young queer people were finding each other before they'd spent a lifetime twisting themselves into something they weren't. The 'net made it easier to learn about queer identities in other cultures and other times, and the bright light of that knowledge cast our own system of sex and gender into harsh relief. On Usenet groups and early weblogs, new labels were birthed and killed a thousand times over, until slowly we worked our way to the fifty-eight gender options that Facebook started to offer in 2014. Gen Z came of age in a world where they could be queer without having to squish themselves into the "gay" box. It's no wonder they are our queerest, bi-est, trans-est generation yet.

I hope they're just getting started.

Eventually I hared off in a new direction, exploring in my late twenties and thirties all the kinds of masculinity I had previously avoided, from punk fag to cishet daddy. I enjoyed it all, just as much as I had my decade of femininity, but I felt obscurely like I had betrayed something. Had I simply given in to what the world wanted of me? It was hard to ignore how much nicer people were when I looked like a guy, and it made me angry.

The more normie I looked, the more important it felt to step into every room with my faggiest foot first. It kept people on their toes and made the assholes obvious. But I felt a strange shame at times, not over who I was but who I wasn't any longer. How could I be *anything* if I refused to be *one* thing?

So I zipped the Ithaca period of my life closed. It was easy to do that back then, when we had no permanent digital selves and only the few photos that someone gave us when they got free duplicates from the film-processing place at the mall. Every once in a while, I'd break out those old pics as a kind of party trick—*gee willikers, get a look at her, eh?* For the most part, though, I let that old self slip into obscurity, as though I had been an expat in a country that no longer existed—not exactly ashamed but exhausted by all the years of living in translation. But it was those years that made me; showed me the world and who I was in it; and blessed me with a brilliant trans community (even if we didn't realize it at the time).

Somedays I wonder who I would have been had I been born twenty years later. An enby, perhaps? A trans woman? Me, exactly as I am now, but terminally online and insufferably Gen Z? I'll never know.

But who doesn't have thoughts about what might have been? Each generation changes the world, creating the spaces and ideas the next will inhabit, but despite our best efforts, we're a product of the context we grew up in. The labels I'd have embraced in my teens and twenties sit awkwardly in my mouth now; I look about as bearded and binary as possible. I think a lot about Judith Butler's idea of gender being *performative*—not that we're pretending but that we create gender every day, through what we do, and it agglutinates to us, in us, over time. I've spent years not telling this story, worried that I'll be labeled a "detransitioner" and my experience will be used as a cudgel against some other young queer person—*see, he didn't need X or Y or Z.* Better never to talk about myself at all. I've always been comfortable in the indeterminacy of silence. Besides, up until 2014, when *Time* magazine declared the so-called Transgender Tipping Point, the realm of people I could have a nuanced conversation with about gender was tiny.

But it's impossible to explain how I see the world without explaining the vantage I come from, uncomfortable though it makes me. The histories that I write today are only possible because of who I was thirty years ago. The worm that eats away at me and tells me I am unreal is still there some mornings, but I whisper back, *We are all unreal.*

I am still in motion, endlessly, effortlessly. Even if I stopped, the fact of changing would always be part of me, like a tree carrying the memory of every forest fire or bountiful spring in its rings. We are all four-dimensional beings—bodies hurtling through time—and everything we *are* is made up of what we *were* and contains the seeds of everything we can become.

Fuck or Fuck Up

I ONLY REMEMBER ONE TEST I TOOK AT CORNELL, BECAUSE I took it over and over again: the Enzyme-Linked Immunosorbent Assay, or ELISA, the first widely available, mostly accurate test for HIV. Between 1996 and 2002, when I left Ithaca for New York City, I tested about every other month, maybe thirty, forty times in total.

Growing up Catholic, the ritual of regularly expiating my sins by confessing them to a stranger made sense to me, and I much preferred Roz (the silver-haired, smoky-voiced butch who ran Cornell's sexual health services) to Father Tim, our ascetic parish priest who looked like a pious Ichabod Crane. I never tested positive, though once I had an ambiguous test that had to be confirmed negative by a secondary test—the Western blot—and those were some of the scariest weeks of my life.

Weeks. At the time I took my first HIV test, it took twenty-one days to get the results.

But AIDS had been part of my life for many years by that point. Starting around 1988, at the age of ten, I had a recurring nightmare in which I was dying of AIDS during a nuclear winter.

I didn't know what "nuclear winter" meant, or—really—what it meant to die of AIDS, but both were regular features on the news, which I watched every night with my grandmother, and so they wormed their way into my brain, which in sleep transmogrified those fears into a gentle scene of ice skaters on a pond in a snowstorm, except the snow was gray, and the skaters were monstrously deformed, and the pond was set in a blackness that went on forever without ground or stars.

I wasn't a person in this dream; I *was* the dream. I was the pond, the poison snow, and the skaters who looked like the caricature puppets from that British TV show *Spitting Image*. The dream was quiet and inevitable and terrifying. The puppets pirouetted on the ice, and I knew somehow that meant that I—the "I" that was the dream—was dying of AIDS. The snow drifted softly, and I was dying of AIDS. Everything else in the world was gone, my life was shaped like a pyramid hurtling toward this moment, and I was dying of AIDS. During a nuclear winter.

I had this dream so often that eventually it stopped being sad or scary and became an unpleasant acquaintance I simply spent a little time with now and again. But it's the only dream I remember from my childhood, and still to this day I can conjure up those doleful skaters and that black pond and feel the certitude of death creep my spine.

I was ten.

Every fag I went to college with dreamed the same dream, though our particulars varied. We were a limbo generation: sexually mature after the hell of the 1980s but well into middle age before the promised land of PrEP came about. Growing up before HIV was a manageable condition, we knew no differentiations: HIV equaled AIDS equaled death. I think most of us assumed we'd get it eventually; I know I did.

AIDS was the only story we had in the '80s. We could discuss gay people in school if they had AIDS. Gays could be on the news if they had AIDS. Straight actors could win Oscars playing gay characters *if* they had AIDS. We had AIDS quilts and ribbons and funds; Days of Rage and Days Without Art; Broadway Cared and Equity Fought and LifeCycled and AIDS AIDS AIDS AIDS AIDS. All we had was AIDS.

We all had AIDS.

That's what it felt like, though of course we didn't. People with AIDS had AIDS; the rest of us had the presumption of AIDS, stitched to us like a second shadow.

The first time a doctor accused me of having AIDS, I was twenty-one with a shitty boyfriend named Rigatoni (guess what his mother was eating when she went into labor) who cheated on me and gave me crabs. My body hair was coarse and patchy and looked like it would keep you warm in the winter; it was also an ideal hiding place for wily lice. I had no idea what was going on, as the itch spread from my balls to my taint and down my thighs.

The overworked nurse at the clinic said something about a rash and gave me a cream; by the time I returned a week later, the little monsters had spread to every fucking follicle on my body, and I was a scratchy mess. This time I got to see the doctor, who looked at me for 0.4 seconds before declaring I had one of two viruses and he needed to do a biopsy immediately. He circled one of the itchiest spots on my arm with a Sharpie, got me on the exam table, and left to prep.

Under the harsh interrogation lights of the exam room, the sad solo crab on my arm—so far from his many friends in Genital City—packed his bags and took off. As I watched him cross the Sharpie line the doctor had drawn, I realized what was happening. I felt disgusting and, more than anything, stupid.

The doctor was furious when I explained what I had seen. Everything about him narrowed—his lips, his eyes, his heart—and he walked out of the room. A few minutes later he returned, holding the paperwork from my first visit.

This was not his fault.

He was anxious to impress that on me. He had never seen a case of crabs this advanced. Something was wrong.

He looked significantly at my paperwork and waited, but I had no idea what he was waiting for. I agreed: Something *was* wrong! I had been misdiagnosed, and now I was a full-body playground for pubic lice.

"This says you work at the gay center at Cornell," the doctor spoke slowly, as though I were a stupid child. "Are you . . . " he waited again for me to speak, and when I didn't, he stumbled awkwardly around what he wanted to say, before landing on "immuno . . . compromised?"

I understood many things in that moment: that he thought I had AIDS because he now knew I was gay; that the parasite on my skin had nothing to do with whether or not I had AIDS; and that he was angry, because he was embarrassed, because he had nearly performed unnecessary surgery on me.

But what I said was "Are you asking if I have leukemia?"

The person I'd been just a second ago—the person who was so embarrassed by his spectacular case of pubic lice—had been incinerated by rage. It wasn't just that I'd been misdiagnosed or that he was an asshole; it was his childish refusal to say the word *AIDS*, the game he was trying to get me to play, the way he wanted me to confess, as though it were a sin and not a syndrome. If he wanted me to say, "I'm sorry, I have AIDS, that's why you were wrong," he was going to be waiting until the end of time, and that was fine with me. I didn't have AIDS, but I was never going to tell him that.

We sat in furious silence until finally, spontaneously, he left. A nurse gave me a prescription for some Agent Orange–esque chemical, which cleared the playing field overnight, and I didn't go to a doctor again for four years, until I got a case of walking pneumonia so bad my boss said I couldn't come in until I got it checked out.

During my years of testing, the AIDS crisis changed in a dramatic yet subtle way: With the advent of retroviral protease inhibitors in 1996, we downshifted into what scholars Ted Kerr and Alexandra Juhasz have named "the second silence." The first silence was that imposed from the top by our crypt-keeper-in-chief, Ronnie Reagan, who refused to even say *AIDS* for most of the Eighties. The second silence was a more organic quieting, as effective drugs, death, and exhaustion turned the volume down. The crisis continued (and still does today), but it was no longer the mobilizing center for the queer community or the only story we were allowed to tell about ourselves. Thousands of people dedicated their lives to fighting AIDS in one of the most effective direct action movements America has ever seen. While 1996 was not the end of the crisis (especially if you were poor, or trans, or Black), for many people it was the first time they could put their burdens down since June 1981, when the initial report about AIDS was published by the Centers for Disease Control and Prevention. After fifteen years of screaming—in anger, in pain, and in loss—they were owed some quiet.

Becoming an adult in those years was like walking into a room that had just been evacuated, with a few dazed survivors wandering around and a broken klaxon blaring in the corner. We were juiced on fear and had no idea what to do about it. Our role models—the ones who lived—had spent the last decade ping-ponging between protests and funerals; what did they know about dating in a post-Ellen-coming-out world?

AIDS receded into the background. But the fear stayed. At best, we'd found a pause button that separated HIV from AIDS and death; at worst, we feared that in three years we'd discover something awful about protease inhibitors, and the world would collapse around us again. And that was my rational mind talking; on an instinctual level, there was no decoupling sex from death in the screaming of my adrenal glands. I could have been mummified in latex while a virgin jerked off in the next room, and I'd still have gone to get tested.

But because my fears were irrational, my behaviors were as well. Months of persnickety protection—dental dams for rimming!—would be broken by nights of rawdogging lawlessness. The guys I was hooking up with were all riding the same yo-yo, all surfing the edge of the inevitable. Some of them died. A few of AIDS, but most through a mix of drugs, alcohol, poverty, suicide, and general lack of care. Players dropped out; the game continued. We were artists, pharmacists, waiters, students, stockboys, delivery guys, trust fund kids; we were excited, hungry, lonely, scared, empowered, embittered; we were—and then some of us weren't.

Although I was undoubtedly having sex with men who were positive, it was mostly unknowing—our mouths were too busy for much conversation. Our negotiations around safer sex were brief and focused on what we were going to do, not why we were going to do it. AIDS was like Bloody Mary: to say its name too often was to summon it into the room. We were adults making adult choices, but we were also children covering our eyes so the monster couldn't see us. In public, I chanted the ACT UP slogan "Silence equals death," but in private, I was tongue-tied.

The longer I was in New York City, the more risky sex I had and the less I talked about it. In the space between what I was doing and what I could acknowledge, the certainty that I'd get AIDS grew stronger. It felt like the door between me and rest of my life, and I was tired of waiting. I wasn't a bugchaser, but I knew a few, and I think the biggest difference between us was they had their eyes open. If we were all going to get AIDS anyway—which we all believed—why not get it over with? And the forbidden nature of unprotected sex made "going raw" an aphrodisiac that some men bonded over in the same way others did with BDSM or fisting. We all just wanted a way out of the fear we'd been born into. Either I'd find my way out, or it would find me, but I knew what I was doing was unsustainable.

That's when Yo came into my life: a beautiful, long-haired, fey man-child whom I'd accidentally ended up dating. The sex was phenomenal, so after a few weeks, we stopped using condoms (without talking about it, of course), and if we hooked up with other people, we didn't talk about that either. Our relationship was far more physical than it was verbal. And I don't just mean sexual. On our first date, he rented a sander and refinished the floors in his newly legal loft in one of the "hipster hives" that had sprung up in Brooklyn after the East Village got too expensive for bohemian living. We went out dancing all the time—in fact, we met on the dance floor, when he walked past me wearing a fox tail attached to his belt and I stroked it instinctively. We made hot, space-themed porn for an indie queer film festival; he was the fugitive Robottom and I the Faggotron 3000 sent to capture him. (On IMDB, I am still improperly identified as "Hughbot," if anyone knows how to fix that.) I can't remember much we ever talked about, aside from plans for the sprawling Robottom cinematic fisting universe.

You know, dating.

But we soon broke a cardinal rule of casual relationships: We went on vacation together, camping at a Radical Faerie homestead in Tennessee. Two weeks in a tent in a place where he had lots of old friends and I knew no one. What could go wrong?

The land where we were camping had been home to a tune-in, dropout hippie commune in the '70s—the kind of place whose denizens had the date of the revolution circled on their calendars, and when it didn't come to pass, most of them quickly tuned back into society. Only the queer folks—the "Radical Faeries"—stayed behind, and over the years, others joined them, slowly buying up unwanted land that was too stony to farm and too mountainous to log, creating a network of queer homes and communes spread across the mountaintop like a patchwork quilt.

In this, they were inspired by Harry Hay, one of America's most important queer community organizers. Hay founded the Mattachine Society, the first significant gay rights group in America, in 1950. But he was soon forced out for his Communist radicalism, and Mattachine became a more centrist (though still important) force in gay organizing. Hay drifted further left, becoming a gay liberationist in the early Seventies, then getting involved in consciousness-raising groups, before founding the Radical Faeries as a rural alternative for gay men who wanted to throw off the shackles of society and connect with nature, sexuality, and each other.

This kind of utopianism was everywhere in the 1970s. All around the country, "women's lands" were springing up, creating ecofeminist paradises that were literal no-man's-lands, while in urban places, gay anarchists were extolling communal living as a political choice and a rejection of the heteronuclear family. Sylvia Rivera and Marsha P. Johnson launched STAR (Street Transvestite Action Revolutionaries) House in NYC's East Village, while The Furies created a lesbian separatist commune in DC that eventually led to the founding of Olivia Records, the OG women's music label in the United States.

Of course, queer people have always moved in together as a form of protection and community, but as with everything else post-Stonewall, the interjection of pride was new. This wasn't a forced choice made because we had been abandoned by our families. These communes were our laboratories for the future, where queer people were creating better ways to live, in harmony with nature and each other. For the most part, these projects didn't last long, but the Radical Faeries managed to hold on, maintaining and even growing their community as many others folded over the years.

Most of the folks who first moved to this particular land in Tennessee were queer men, now over the age of forty, many of them long-term AIDS survivors. There was neither cell phone service nor Wi-Fi, but there was a wood-heated bathhouse, and visitors were welcome if they brought a tent and were willing to pitch in. A few times a year, the Faeries planned large gatherings that brought two or three hundred visitors from around the world; Yo and I were there for Beltane, a pagan spring ceremony complete with a ritual maypole raising.

Yo ran into one of his exes the first night we were there, a globe-trotting party promoter named Jaguar. The second night, he never came back to our tent, and the next day we officially broke up. Our relationship had mostly been shallow, sexy fun, and while I was sad it was over, I wasn't heartbroken, and I knew we'd be friends again on the far side of things. But I was very confused about how I was going to spend the next week and a half, since I knew basically no one else on the mountain.

Before this, I'd spent a little time in intergenerational queer spaces—the line for the bathroom at the gay bar; the L train after 11 p.m. on a Friday; brunch—but I'd never really gotten to know a lot of queer men older than me. A whole bunch *were* dead, so there was that. But also, I didn't like older men in general. They were usually misogynistic, often both controlling and completely unaware of their effects on others, and always in power. If I blurred my eyes, every person in a position of authority seemed to be the same White guy. I'd had some of the best sex of my life with older men (some of the worst too), but I drew the line at talking with them.

Except now I was alone, on a mountain, with a couple hundred of them. I wasn't the youngest person at the gathering, but I wasn't far off either.

For my entire life, my parent's house had been the designated family party place, because my grandmother lived there and it was large enough to host fifty people at once. So I had a script for handling big gatherings where I felt out of place: Go to the kitchen, find the oldest woman, and offer to help.

Simmer was around my age, but it was clear she was in charge (of the kitchen, of the universe) from the moment we met. I'd learn later that six months out of the year, she was a baker on a ship that did river work for the Army Corp of Engineers. She was a fierce blend of earth witch and drill sergeant who could turn out a vegan dinner for 400 without breaking a sweat—and have it taste great too. Everything about her radiated Big Dyke Energy, from her wild mullet to her work-muddied Carhartt's. During the gatherings, the kitchen was volunteer run, and Simmer ran the volunteers.

It was early morning, and she put me to work making coffee, a process that involved a propane burner so big it looked like the Eye of Sauron and a pot of water I could have bathed in. Once the pot was full, I couldn't lift it by myself, so I gathered a few of the postparty wraiths—those quiet dawn drifters who can't go to bed but aren't quite awake either—and collectively we got the coffee perking.

"What now?" I asked Simmer, who seemed surprised I'd returned. I handed her a cup of fresh coffee, and she shook her head with a laugh.

"Oh no, girl, no," she murmured, and steered me down a narrow set of steps to the basement pantry, where she'd hidden a tiny espresso maker. "Workers get the good stuff."

Two shots later, she set me to peeling carrots. A literal mountain's worth. I peeled carrots until the carrot peels surrounded me in a giant, orange, curly peel pile, like I'd shaved Little Orphan Annie. Then I think she set me to cracking hundreds of eggs—I know she didn't trust me, on that first day, to do something as complicated as chop onions. She had lived on the land for years and was accustomed to the gatherings being full of lovely but easily distracted people, who'd volunteer to help but then never return from washing their hands. I was straight edge, six hours single, and knew basically no one on the land other than Yo; once Simmer understood I was both lonely and reliable, she scooped me under her wing. I lived in the kitchen for the rest of the gathering . . . and for all the gatherings I went to for the next ten years.

The kitchen was a hippie's wet dream: a vast open space with two parallel rows of prep tables, two industrial stoves (one with a bread oven), several lounging couches, a ginormous basement pantry, a cold storage trap in a nearby stream, and innumerable glass jars of bulk grains, spices, teas, tinctures, tisanes, remedies, and concoctions. One clock was permanently set to 4:20; the other had no hands.

The kitchen is always the heart of the party, and that holds true even when the party is a pagan ritual spread across a hundred acres of Tennessee mountaintop. People wandered in and out all day long, looking for snacks, hot water for tea, or (like me) a place to plug in when they felt untethered. Faerie land was amazing but also overpowering, and many folks were drawn to the gatherings because they had no access to community like this in their day-to-day lives: no place to be out, to dress as they wanted, to meet other queer people, to party in a community that would take care of them if they had a bad trip, etc. If you were sleepy, or sad, or fucked up, or lonely, the kitchen was the reliable place to find sober(ish) people who'd give you a job to do or a shoulder to cry on (or, if we needed onions that day, both). I've never been great at relaxing—I enjoy parties most when I'm working them—but perhaps as a result, I'm very good at making chores fun. Kitchen witch, it turned out, was my calling. And my calling card: I met basically every single person on the mountain, one at a time, over a plate of massaged kale with lemon, tahini, and nutritional yeast dressing.

Most nights, after dinner the kitchen turned into a spontaneous dance party. The prep tables were cleared out when the janky old stereo went on, or people just got up and danced on them. One of the privileges of working in the kitchen was choosing the music, at least until some queen who was also a famous DJ woke up from her disco nap and took over (this literally happened to me more than once). Back in New York, I'd taken a side gig working for a crappy straight boy music magazine out of Boston; I wrote reviews of whatever CDs they sent me, which were also my paychecks. The job fell apart when the head editor experienced an abrupt religious conversion and sent out an email saying we could no longer review albums he considered immoral. But before that, as I packed for Tennessee, they sent me an album I thought was genuinely great: *Frank*, by an unknown singer named Amy Winehouse. It wasn't even released in the United States yet.

Let me tell you this: There is no greater one-night god than the one who descends a new diva on the gayborhood.

"In My Bed" (track 8) was blasting when Antoine walked in. He had long, feathered red hair, expressive eyebrows that darted around like sparrows when he was surprised, and what was then a telltale sign of being a long-term AIDS survivor: wiry limbs with an unexpectedly round stomach. Some of the early drugs had a way of redistributing the fat on your body, skinnying your arms and thickening your belly, and in loud, dark, half-naked spaces, it was as reliable a sign of being HIV positive as the then ubiquitous biohazard tattoos.

"Who-ooo is thiiii-iis?" Antoine's eyebrows flew up and down, following his voice, which fluted like Snagglepuss exiting stage left.

I tossed him the CD case, and we got to talking. A decade older than me, he was an artist of a dozen stripes, a writer/musician/filmmaker/dancer. He was also a progressive politics junkie with mainstream Democrat leanings, something that was rather rare at the gathering, where people were often too spiritual, too radical, or too lazy for electoral politics. We soon found ourselves talking about the relative strengths of the Democratic field shaping up for the 2004 election. Bush was toast, *everyone* could see that, so now the Democratic primary was the real contest.

We were of course Deaniacs, because he was the leftiest of the mainstream candidates. No one with a shot in hell at becoming president supported gay rights in a meaningful way in 2004. Even Howard Dean equivocated, sucking up to evangelicals by staying mum about his personal beliefs while saying that the Democratic platform defined marriage as a union between a man and a woman—and *still*, he seemed like the most viable, gay-friendly candidate. The first presidential hopeful to support gay marriage on the campaign trail was Barack Obama in 2012—and even then it was only because Joe Biden, his VP pick, forced his hand. Dean's tepid homophobia was downright progressive compared to his party at the time. But we couldn't have predicted that in a few months he would commit the unforgiveable sin of yelling, "Yeah!" after coming in third in the Iowa primary and be banished to the political wilderness for eternity.

Antoine and I drifted closer on the couch, my hands finding their way to his hair, which I stroked with a guilty touch as he curled into me like a sassy lion, all teased mane and soft underbelly. We made out, stopped, started again.

"I—I can't do this." I began to explain about Yo, the breakup, and the fact that we were still *maybe* sharing a tent, even though I hadn't seen him in days. Antoine put one long finger to my lips and rolled his eyes.

"Shhhh-shhh-shh," he quieted me. "It's the Mountain," he purred. "That shit happens your first time. Sometimes every time." He put his head on my chest. "Doesn't matter anyway though, playground's closed for remodeling!"

I looked at him quizzically.

"Herps outbreak on my hoo-ha. Oh, and just so you know, I've got the AIDS."

He was shockingly casual about it. Well, casual isn't the right word—he did a big sparkle-fingers gesture as he said it, as though in postprocessing the word *AIDS* would swoop across the screen in bubble letters. But still, he treated it as though it were just the name of a disease and not an incantation for doom.

He went to kiss me, and I pulled away reflexively, still thinking about Yo.

"That's a lower-hole problem," he whispered, and his tongue darted out and licked my lip, ridiculously. I couldn't help but laugh, and then we were making out again. There was an ease to knowing nothing else was going to happen, not right away at least, and we spent the rest of our time in Tennessee acting like middle school sweethearts. (Or at least, what I imagined middle school sweethearts acted like, since I had no actual experience to draw from or even TV relationships to ape.) We talked about what we would do, one day, and those fantasies were hotter than most hookups I'd had (also Antoine gave great head). Not once did I wake up the next morning convinced I had AIDS, despite the fact that the boogeyman of my nightmares was in my mouth the night before.

Immediately after getting back from Tennessee, I got a shitty (literal) stomach bug, and then work was crazy, and then

I was still sad about Yo and me breaking up, and then one day I realized I hadn't had sex in weeks, and it had been . . . relaxing. The fear, which touched anything that touched sex—including not having sex—rushed in: *You're not gonna stay celibate forever. Give up now, get it over with!*

But in the reflection of my week with Antoine, I saw how nonsensical that was. My fear of AIDS was pushing me to do the very things that put me at higher risk, because I was in a permanent, unacknowledged state of panic, which made logical thought impossible. The fear wasn't protecting me; it was driving me to the same conclusion I'd been told my whole life: that AIDS was my inevitable end. Antoine had broken the illogical syllogisms in my head. HIV did not equal death, and talking about AIDS wouldn't make me positive. But these were weak, newborn truths—revelations I didn't yet know what to do with. I needed time away from my fear to sit with them; time like I'd had in Tennessee.

Summoning Antoine's cool and the taste of him on my lips, I muttered to myself, *Playground's closed*.

That was it. No grand plan. The easiest way to make a new choice was to take my usual order off the menu entirely. For Antoine, celibacy was a practical, time-limited strategy to use when sex would not be good for him or the person he was with. I decided to follow *his* lead, listen to *his* voice instead of the ones in my head, and see where that went.

At first, I demurred guiltily, breaking away mid-make-out at a bar to mumble apologies and speed off. But that made me feel like the half-closeted guys I hooked up with in college, and soon I found it easier to say upfront that I wasn't having sex at the moment. Some guys evaporated like dry ice the moment my dick was off the table; others seemed relieved. A few asked questions, and eventually I started answering them. Because the stakes were low—because the playground was closed—it was easier to discuss what turned me on or off and what risks I wanted to take. It gave me time to practice.

In high school, I'd rolled my eyes at my straight friends' endless, sexless dating; the hours of processing with their significant others, who were obviously not all that significant; the breakups over nothing. It was dumb, I thought, deeply dumb, not realizing that the dumbness was the point. Low stakes, lots of fuckups: That's how we learn. But young queer people rarely get that grace, even today. Either we're not out until we're older, or there's no one around to make mistakes with. We never learn how to fuck or fuck up. At least not when our peers are doing it. Instead, we learn as adults, without a safety net, and blame ourselves and each other when we fall.

What was I afraid of, all those years? When I think back on that black pond and that old dream now, I'm struck by what wasn't in it: Sex. Gay people. My body. The dream was ignorance and loneliness made metaphor. I thought it was inevitable that I'd die because of AIDS, when it was inevitable that I'd die because I was human. But AIDS was the only story I was given, so it was the story I told about myself, even before I knew what it was—or who I was—or who any one positive was. I was cowering beneath a giant shadow, but when I looked directly at it, AIDS was so much smaller than I thought: a disease caused by a virus 100 nanometers around. I wasn't destined to get it, and if I got it, I wasn't destined to die from it, and if I did die from it, that could be in two years or seventy, and those years could be good or bad or—like most—some of each.

No, I wasn't afraid of AIDS; I was afraid of a world that said AIDS was all I had to look forward to. So of course it took getting away from that world, even just to the unwanted side of a mountain in Tennessee, for me to see what that fear really was. Thank God for men with AIDS: They saved me from myself and what the world had twisted me into. They showed me how ridiculous my fears were and how great life could be on the other side of those fears. They taught me to use my tongue—in more ways than one.

After six months of celibacy, I went back to having sex. I did all the same things I'd done before, but everything felt different with my eyes (and mouth) open. I turned testing into an adventure and tried every free clinic New York City had to offer. Some mornings I woke up to find my sheets soaked with sweat, and the old fears whispering in my head, but those moments became rarer and rarer, until one day, during a physical decades later, my doctor offered me an HIV test, and I realized I'd been with my partners for years and couldn't remember the last time I'd taken one. The version of me that roamed the tea rooms and testing centers of Cornell imagined getting AIDS and not getting AIDS, dying and not dying; but the thing I never anticipated at age twenty was that one day I wouldn't think about AIDS much at all.

Never Let School Get in the Way of Your Education

ON WHAT WAS SUPPOSED TO BE THE SECOND DAY OF MY senior year at Cornell, I was reading *Das Kapital* on a Greyhound bus parked in a travel plaza somewhere in Illinois when God sent me a message: "Never let school get in the way of your education," picked out in leftover plastic letters, just below the two-for-one meal deal on the Wendy's sign.

I was a little lost in those days, always looking for signs to point me in a new direction because I no longer seemed to have a direction of my own. And it seemed like good advice (by which I mean it confirmed what I'd already decided to do), so I shoved *Das Kapital* deep into the bottom of my backpack, past my hot-pink fake-fur vest, my silver lamé skirt-pants, my sleeping bag, my water bottle, the Australian Driza-Bone hat that made me feel like Indiana Jones, and the dirty Tupperware that had until recently held the chickpea chili I'd stolen from Cornell's dining hall to fuel my fifty-four-hour bus ride from Buffalo, New York, to Reno, Nevada. It was August 1999; Y2K was on its way to destroy the information superhighway; and I was skipping the first few weeks of my senior year to go to Burning Man.

Sort of.

Like most schools, Cornell had an extended add/drop period at the start of each term, and I'd realized I could skip all my classes and tell my professors I'd been shopping around when I returned. I wasn't lazy; I was efficient. If some students didn't need those first few weeks, why did any of us?

In fact, why go back at all? whispered the pigtailed demon on the Wendy's sign.

I'd spent the summer in Washington, DC, working as an organizer with the Progressive Party. For eight hours a day, I stood by a pay phone with a roll of quarters, trying to convince passersby to tell their city council member to vote for our living wage bill. The bill was doomed, and far from making a living wage, I made so little money I was living on couches, dumpster diving pastries for breakfast. But it gave me a place to be that summer, when Cornell was closed and I didn't want to go home because my parents and I were constantly arguing. Surprisingly, I loved the job. It worked muscles I'd let atrophy at school, like how to have a conversation without citing Foucault. Here, my raver-hippie affect worked in my favor, drawing to me the vivacious, unhinged folks who were likely to say, "*Yes*,

I do want to use my lunch break to yell at a stranger's answering machine."

After the first week, it dawned on me: My job wasn't really to get people to make calls; it was to get them to believe their opinions mattered. In class, conversations about ideas were mostly sparring matches, all about ripping each other apart to find the weakness in our arguments. Even the teachers could be cruel. One semester, I was taking a small seminar with a professor I'll call Jones, a celebrated lesbian feminist, who taught the most radical classes on race, politics, economics, and gender. Her reading lists opened me up to everyone from James Baldwin to Lata Mani. She was brilliant and accomplished, and I lived in terror of ever attracting her attention. She was in a constant state of frozen fury, as though you had personally insulted her years ago, and she was now biting her tongue so you could work together. Her look was pure '90s power lesbian: pants, vests, and blazers, with shoulder-length hair that somehow emphasized the severeness of her demeanor instead of softening it. She liked me, and I don't think that mattered at all.

Our seminar only had ten people in it, and a few of us were required to give presentations each week. Early on, a student named Cheryl screwed up during her presentation; said "heteronormativity" when she meant "performativity," or some other obvious slip of the tongue. Professor Jones was in a bad mood, and she leaped on the mistake, batting Cheryl about, asking her why that word, what it meant in this context, and how it would apply to this scholar or that. I think if Cheryl had gone belly up like a scared dog, Jones would have gotten bored, but she made the mistake of trying to defend herself. For the next fifteen minutes, Jones tortured her with questions, until Cheryl cried and left the room. Then Jones looked slowly around the seminar table, meeting our eyes one by one. "Come prepared," she said icily and walked out. Cheryl quit the class; the rest of us did nothing. I don't think it even occurred to me to ask if she was OK.

Literary criticism, critical theory, writing crits—everything ran on a model of critique first, common ground second.

On the street, campaigning for a living wage, that didn't work; the people who disagreed with me just walked away, and if I was an asshole, I lost the ones who agreed with me too. My job was to talk *with* them, not *at* them. If they made a call at the end, great! But if not, there was still one more person out there who had a better idea of what a living wage was and what the Progressive Party did—and I had a better sense of their lives and what they wanted from a party that claimed to represent the people. My sidewalk ministry wasn't going to turn anyone socialist over lunch, but I could connect their fears and frustrations with potential solutions. I loved having a job that was so small and tangible. I measured my days in change: quarters, minds.

But the best part of the job was that my friend Laura lived in the Virginia suburbs, and through her I met Morgan, my first serious boyfriend. He was an eighteen-year-old bisexual high school dropout hacker—basically the coolest thing you could be in the '90s. He was always developing some grand plan and shocking everyone when he saw it through. He was the platonic ideal of the slacker: lazy, yet somehow ahead of everybody else, or really to the side of everybody else, doing his own thing. In a very queer fashion, I wanted to *be* him as much as I wanted to be with him. (Queer people don't carry the baggage of constantly being told that our ideal partner is also our absolute opposite; that in order to find love we'll need to traverse distances measured in the light-years between Mars and Venus. Instead, we get to worry about rampant narcissism causing us to look no further than the mirror when falling in love—a way of doubling your wardrobe and ego at the same time.)

Morgan helped me set up my first "web log" (which eventually got shorted to "blog"), and in return I took his virginity on the bed in my boss's guest room in Anacostia. We invented sex that summer, in fact, and spent many hours—sometimes entire weekends—holed up in his suburban bedroom trying out new permutations. He was naturally submissive, and that made me feel safe. I loved slowly making him cum, seeing how long we could wait. We were both skinny and long-haired with an occasional penchant for skirts; it was equal odds if any given asshole would call us "faggots" or "dykes." (No one ever called us trannies, though, because that was still mostly an in-group barbed compliment back then—I love *Project Runway* and Christian Siriano, but I'll never forgive them for introducing straight people to the term.)

As my job came to a close and I prepared to head back to Ithaca, Morgan mentioned this weird festival in the desert. I'd never heard of it, but I didn't want our summer to be over, and I *really* didn't want to go back to school, not after the way junior year had ended. I was looking to make some new mistakes.

Burning Man was not then what it is now. Outside weirdo techie artists on the West Coast, it had little public profile. It had only started in 1986, when it was just a group of close friends—artists who made and destroyed art to celebrate the renewal rituals of the summer solstice. As it grew, it became a "temporary autonomous zone" (a phrase defined by queer theorist Hakim Bey in his 1991 book of the same title)—a place that was consciously intended to be a short-lived experiment in a different way of living. It was an idea that caught fire in the preppy and conformist era of the late Eighties, when Burning Man began to balloon. The 25,000-person crowd I'd encounter in 1999 seemed unfathomably large; I can't imagine what it felt like in 2023, when 75,000 people showed up.

I don't know for sure what has changed in those years, except that when I was there, the cost of going was so much lower, the crowd seemed genuinely mixed (in terms of class; it was really White even back then). Since 2013, the organizers have collected population reports to understand who goes to Burning Man, and the data shows, more than anything, that the crowd has gotten wealthier and wealthier over the years. In 2013, people with an income of more than $100,000 made up about 20 percent of attendees; ten years later, it was 40 percent. That year, the most expensive last-minute tickets were $3,000, but after those sold out, a lucrative black market sprung up, where the global elite paid up to $10,000 to get in.

In 1999, Morgan and I bought our tickets a week before the Burn for the exorbitant price of $99. It felt like kismet when we discovered that Greyhound was offering an end-of-summer promotion: $99 for a round-trip ticket anywhere in the continental

United States. What little information we could find about Burning Man said things like “Bring a gallon of water per person per day,” but we were pretty sure we could work around that. Ignorance and guesswork were the spice of life in those proto-internet, pre–cell phone days. Unexpected delights were ours to discover, and environmental and ethical concerns were easy to miss.

So at the end of August, I stopped by Cornell for a day, told everyone I was shopping around, snapped up my syllabuses, and headed to Buffalo to ride the ’Hound.

The only problem was that one of my professors required that I write a paper about everything on the syllabus I’d be missing. Her class was the only one I absolutely needed, an upper-level women’s studies seminar that met a necessary requirement I’d yet to clear.

And that was how I found myself reading *Das Kapital* in the travel plaza, beneath the watchful eyes of Wendy, thirty hours outside Reno. As the bus gassed up, I scribbled out a few pages, longhand, on spiral-bound notebook paper, then made an envelope out of duct tape (I always had duct tape on me in those years; it could patch your jeans, shoes, or arm in a jiffy), stuffed the paper inside, and dropped it in the mail.

Even then, part of me wondered if I was ever going back.

At the start of my junior year, months before my Burning Man folly, I’d received another surprising communiqué from above: Some office of academic achievement had reached out to urge me to apply for one of the big postgraduate fellowships,

Rhodes, Truman, Marshall, etc. They suggested I pick one to focus on and that I treat the application like another class in my schedule.

I couldn't imagine winning a Rhodes scholarship—that was a thing people did in movies. But the Truman Scholarship was all about the intersection of politics and public service, what I had recently learned was *praxis*, the place where theory met practice. That was what I wanted: to use my mind to be of useful service, somehow.

My grades were good—I had just below a 4.0—but I knew what really distinguished me was everything else: A professor had asked to publish one of my papers in a book she was working on; I was in a play every semester and was the director of a political theater group; I'd founded a direct action student organization to stop homophobia; I'd been an RA, a TA, and a student rep on the LGB Studies Committee; I'd organized concerts against sexual violence and a Red Cross blood drive to raise awareness about the homophobia of Red Cross blood drives, etc. Increasingly, I saw academia as a way to mix my nerdy passions with my activist inclinations.

I particularly loved what I was learning in women's studies. We were deep in what at the time was called "third-wave feminism." The first wave was the suffragettes, who fought for women's legal equality, like the right to vote; the second wave was the feminists of the '60s and '70s, who fought against gender roles; and here we were, the third wave—the best wave!—bringing it all together to create an intersectional feminism that challenged notions of race, sexuality, gender, the body, class, and so much more. And yes, I mean literally intersectional: I read the article that invented that term (Kimberlé Crenshaw's "Demarginalizing the Intersection of Race and Sex") in at least three classes. This was the height of the riot grrrl years, a punk-inflected moment when the rallying cry "girls to the front" went from being a call for male meatheads to move out of the way at concerts to a more general credo for DIY young feminist organizing. We built collectives against rape and took back the night; we organized womanist study groups and political poetry slams. Scholars like Mimi Nguyen took profound political insights out of their PhD programs and wrote them into carefully folded, aesthetically pleasing zines that we ordered from PO boxes around the country. Feminism changed our lives, and we took those changes right back into vigorous—often acrimonious—classroom debates.

Today, in some states, teachers can be fired for handing out readings that would make White students, like me, uncomfortable, but that discomfort was necessary and productive. It's easy to see the ways in which *we* are disadvantaged—being queer, in fact, helped me to see through a lot of bullshit, like the Republican Party, the Catholic Church, and the later films of Kevin Smith. But it was harder to see my own advantages; how easy, for instance, I found it to talk in seminars because I had spent eighteen years in small classes where almost everyone looked like me and spoke English as a first language. It wasn't lost on me that Cheryl, the only woman of color in our seminar, was the person Professor Jones went after. Even at Cornell, the vast majority of my teachers were White and had received a very similar education to the one I was getting. I was scared of Professor Jones, but I had decades of experience with people like her, and I could reasonably expect that she would see me as—well, not an equal but someone similar to a younger her. That alone gave me a leg up on many students. I should have been able to understand all this simply by looking at the world I lived in, but that's one of the powers of privilege: It obscures the benefits it heaps on you, until you can easily believe that you're simply better, or luckier, than everyone around you. Women's studies freed me. I would rather have been occasionally, productively uncomfortable than spend life as a clueless White man-baby. (And yes, those are the only two options.)

The more I studied, the angrier I became with the very structure of our university in a thousand ways. Why did legacy students get such an advantage in admissions? Because they had rich parents. Why did we have a multi-million-dollar endowment, when so many of my friends were drowning in loans? Why was the Africana Studies Department so far off campus that if you took a class there, they had to give you a free pass for the Ithaca city buses?

(Eventually I learned the answer to that one: Because in 1970 White supremacists had burned the original Africana studies building, and so they moved for their protection—the same reason our one gay bar was so far outside town.)

The thing that infuriated me most, however, was Cornell's Reserve Officer Training Corps (ROTC) program. ROTC students received scholarships in exchange for doing military training and promising to sign up after graduation for a set number of years in the service. The presence of all those student-soldiers made the campus feel like it was occupied by an enemy force. It was an insidious deal for poor students, transforming their college experience into military-lite: They did drills, wore uniforms, took some separate classes, and had to build their future around their required years of service.

For poor queer students, it was even worse. Don't Ask, Don't Tell (DA/DT) was the law of the land—if they came out, they'd be drummed out of ROTC, kicked out of Cornell, and forced to pay back their scholarships. DA/DT was considered a progressive compromise in those days, enacted by a Democratic president on the back of the brutal murder of Petty Officer Allen R. Schindler Jr., who was beaten to death by two other sailors despite his numerous attempts to get the Navy to intervene. Schindler's head was reduced to a pulp; his parents eventually had to identify his body based on the tattoos on his arms. In return, Bill Clinton enacted Don't Ask, Don't Tell in 1993, a way of saying, "Shut the fuck up so we don't have to shut you up again."

During my junior year, Cornell became embroiled in Don't Ask, Don't Tell reform when two ROTC students came forward about death threats they'd received, from both students and officers. Cornell had a nondiscrimination policy, and the administration admitted that DA/DT violated it, but they didn't do anything.

The application for the Truman fellowship asked us to make informed policy recommendations to the US government. I decided I'd focus on ending Don't Ask, Don't Tell. There were other issues I thought were more pressing—the AIDS crisis was still raging all around us, after all—but repealing Don't Ask, Don't Tell was a specific policy change that would have an immediate effect on my community. I thought it would be edgy to the fellowship committee but still within the bounds of the Overton Window in 1998.

I was so naive.

The Greyhound pulled into Reno around midnight, but Morgan wouldn't arrive until the morning, so I spent the night riding escalators in casinos, stealing the snacks left out for the 3 a.m. slot machine addicts.

The Reno welcome sign had been vandalized to read, "The biggest little ~~city~~ shitty in the world," and it tried hard to live up to its motto. Reno felt like a sad, old vampire, a desiccated succubus going through the barest motions of seduction. It aspired to tacky but lacked the joy.

Everything around me felt gray, even the people. I wondered what slow-grinding process had brought these dustmen here rather than to Las Vegas, which at least had glitz, if not actual grandeur. My father and I had recently gotten into a fight about—of all things—shoes, but it wasn't *really* about shoes; it was about my future, or increasingly what seemed to be my lack of one, and how I needed to have good, businessman shoes so I could lead a good, businessman life. A plan, a path—my father wanted to know I was following something, going somewhere. But I wasn't, and shoes weren't going to fix that. They were a stand in for the thing we couldn't talk about, which was, unfortunately, the unparsable knot of my gender and sexuality, which snarled every conceivable life path they (or I) could imagine. College was ending; it was time for me to pick a lane (and shoes to match). Looking around at the dusty shadows perched at the Reno slot machines, I wondered if these men had also drifted too long, let the wind push them around until they finally ended up here, planless, lifeless, hoping only to play the quarter that would save them.

It was a relief to meet Morgan's bus at the station at dawn. He tumbled out sleepy eyed, and I curled myself into the poof of his long, wavy, never-brushed brown hair. Then we pulled apart, wary always of being too affectionate in public, though for once it didn't matter. Overnight the bus station had become bloated with weirdos. For years, it felt like I glowed neon pink every time I walked out in public, but in this room, you couldn't find me with a spotlight. The crowd felt like the anarchic, fabulous, and sometimes spoiled Club Kids I'd met at Limelight and Tunnel. So I took Morgan's hand again carefully, pushed us against his tall camping backpack (which mostly hid us from view), and softly bit the tender spot where his neck met his collarbone, which always made him shiver.

"Let's get this over with," he said after a moment of snuggles. He had a crazy plan for getting us from Reno to the actual Burn, but it required his least favorite thing: talking to strangers. That's where I came in. We surveyed the room, and after a moment, I pointed out a tall, grizzled solo traveler who had electric yellow goggles, a twitchy affect, and two massive camping backpacks he was trying to carry simultaneously.

"Hey, let me help you," I said, and Jeff gratefully handed me one of his bags. After a moment of chatting to ascertain that he was indeed headed to the Burn, we explained Morgan's plan: We needed a car to take all our stuff to the desert, but most people who were driving had a ton of stuff themselves and wouldn't have room for us—or Jeff and his two giant bags. We couldn't rent our own car, because neither Morgan nor I could drive, *and* because we couldn't afford a car for the full week we'd be in the desert. So we convinced Jeff to rent a car that we'd pay for and drive out to the Burn together. Then he'd return the rental while we guarded his stuff and set up camp, and it'd be easy for him to hitch a ride back out, because he wouldn't be carrying anything anymore.

It was a dumb plan full of opportunities to screw each other over, and Jeff went for it instantly.

He started to explain a complicated backstory involving an ex-girlfriend and a baby, who were maybe also headed to Burning Man? I'd been awake for most of the last three days, and honestly, after he agreed to get the car, I stopped listening.

Six hours later, Morgan and I were finally at the Burn. It felt like we'd arrived at the Tina Turner city from *Mad Max: Beyond Thunderdome*—in part because there was an actual Thunderdome, where people dangled from harnesses while fighting with Nerf swords as a DJ remixed house beats with samples from hardcore porn. There was also a fully functional one-screen movie theater shaped like an electrical plug; an amateur *American Gladiators* course; a wandering-bar-slash-pirate-ship where the seats had bicycle pedals that kept the whole thing in constant motion; a twenty-foot spinning, glowing monolith called the Triptonomicon; and a transhumanist cult, founded by obscenely rich software engineers from Seattle, called the Church of Mez.

On the first night, a windstorm wrecked our campsite, Jeff disappeared, and we wandered the desert like two extraneous apostles until in the distance we saw a giant glowing pavilion: the Mezbians. Our sacrilicious saviors.

I dressed up to meet Professor Jones when she called me into her office, as best I could: I wore the long, flowing black pants that a design student had made me for a fashion show, paired with a pristine vintage T-shirt celebrating "Spring Day 1978" (I'd found a whole box of them while cleaning out part of a sub-basement in my job as an RA), and a powder-blue, second-hand, double-breasted vinyl women's raincoat that fit me like a suit jacket from the future. I looked strange but put together, which was generally all I hoped for.

I shouldn't have bothered.

Jones was going to be one of my references for the Truman application, which I'd been working on all semester. Asking her was risky, I knew—she was a Marxist, for God's sake, and Canadian! She didn't want gays serving in the military. But we had very few out professors, and she was the only one whose work was relevant to my application. She said yes immediately, and I glowed for the rest of the day. But that was before she'd seen my topic, so when she emailed me to come to her office hours to discuss the application, the short, formal diction of her message was a message all in itself. I knew I'd disappointed her and that she'd found my application stupid, politically retrograde, and probably a good reason not to accept me into her senior seminar.

Jones's office was chilly, physically and emotionally: small, spare, and white walled, with a large desk facing a single wood-backed chair. She gave me a tight smile when I walked in, her hands already riffling through the pages of my application. We skipped the pleasantries.

Quickly but painstakingly, she cataloged the things she loved about my application, as though making a list of the ways I'd fucked her mother. The research, in particular, impressed her, and she grilled me on it for fifteen confusing minutes. The yawning disconnect between what she was saying and how she was saying it left me reeling, so when she finally stopped, we just sat there in silence. Then Jones lifted the entire pile of pages and dropped them on her desk with a dramatic *thump*.

"*This*," she gestured toward my application like it was a sack of shit, "is fantastic. And it's never going to win."

My heart sunk a little, but she was only saying something I'd already considered. I knew I was taking a big swing, I started to explain, but she cut me off.

"No," she said, frustration snarling her face. "*You* are not going to win. You aren't even going to make it past the campus-wide rounds. No one wants *you*"—her hand stabbed at my outfit, my application, my soul—"to represent Cornell."

I looked at her then, really looked at her: the tight fists balled in her lap, the stress lines on her face, how her whole body seemed to vibrate as if only her blazer were holding her together. I thought about her small, remote office and the way the writers for the conservative student paper routinely mocked her courses without ever taking them. She was brilliant, and very few people cared. She seemed old to me then, but she was so young, I didn't know—just seven years out of her PhD, still an associate professor, up for tenure that year. What compromises had she made to be on the other side of that desk? What had she given away, and in return, had she gotten anything other than anger?

In the late '90s, all "marginalized" disciplines were routinely branded political correctness gone amuck. We had few queer faculty and no out trans faculty at all. Later my junior year, Cornell issued a controversial "ethnic studies report" that recommended shrinking and combining our Africana, Asian American, and Latino studies programs. Student activists were infuriated by the findings but not surprised: The administration hadn't included a single member of those disciplines on the committee that wrote the report. This was genuinely Professor Jones's way of helping me: half a warning of what was to come, half a slap in the face for not knowing it already.

When I realized she was being kind, not cruel, I thanked her and left her office. A few weeks later, Cornell chose some other students for the scholarships. But in the process, they sent my rejection home to my parents, who thus discovered I was majoring in women's studies and threatened to stop paying my tuition. It wasn't the first time. I said fine, hung up on them, and spent the next year wondering if I'd wake up one day to find myself no longer enrolled. I trashed every copy of my application and deleted all the files. I felt foolish—like a fool—like I had fooled myself into believing things that could not be true, the way a child would.

Idiot, I told myself, *you fucking idiot.*

Why had I done all this? Why was I still doing it? A few months earlier, an acquaintance had mentioned that she had wanted to nominate me for Cornell's secret society, Quill and Dagger, but when she did, other members mentioned that I made people uncomfortable, and my nomination was withdrawn. It wasn't that I thought I *deserved* the Truman fellowship or to join the Masons of Ithaca—well, OK, a part of me did; I have a big ego—but mostly I just didn't want to waste myself, to be Charlie Brown, constantly going ass over teakettle while Lucy laughed at me. I didn't want to wake up one day and find myself made of dust and anger.

For a long time, I thought that I was really smart and that that mattered and would magically get me past the hurdles of life and structural oppression. Now I realized that not only did it *not* matter, I was dumb as shit for thinking that it did.

Soon after, when a friend told me he was applying for the Democracy Summer program down in DC, I decided, *Why not?* I had one year left in college, and I knew none of it mattered.

Ambra was holding Morgan's hand while her husband, Stevie, went down on her; they were on the other side of the couch, invisible to us, but they were both moaners, so it wasn't hard to tell what was happening. It was our fifth day living among the Mezbians, and we had become accustomed to our role, which was somewhere between foundlings, pets, and aphrodisiacs. We continued discussing our itinerary for the afternoon (I wanted to find a sculpture we'd heard about, a giant tree made of sun-bleached bones) as Ambra and Stevie climaxed—mutually, which was nice.

The Mezbian compound was filled with couches and costumes and rugs and drugs; bisexual women and heteroflexible men; a generator for power and two giant cold shipping containers, one for food, the other for subzero dance parties. Their pavilion had dozens of tapestries affixed to the roofline on all sides, which could easily be rolled up or down to create walls. On the night of the storm, it looked like a glowing fortress, and when we snuck in, we discovered a wild, tiny party; they'd planned to host their whole neighborhood, but the weather had kept most people cooped up. Their attitude toward the Burn—and life, we would learn—was one of largesse; a party just for themselves was no real party at all, and thus they were delighted to find two windblown desert orphans—Burning Man newbs, no less!—at their otherwise unattended party. "Unattended" except of course for the fifteen or twenty of them. "Stay!" they insisted, plying us with warm food, cold beverages, and a pharmacopeia of drugs for Morgan. We left briefly the next day to recover what was left of our campsite, then moved in with them for the rest of the Burn.

I reclaimed Morgan's hand from Ambra ("Thank you," she purred), and we stepped out into the day. The hard-packed white desert sand reflected the sun at strange angles, making mirages flicker and disappear as we walked, adding to the surreal nature of the event. The barren desert made a perfect backdrop for the density of art all around us, nature's original white box gallery. Every few steps we stopped to admire an amazing outfit, or get lost inside a life-sized game of Mousetrap, or let a naked person inside a giant plastic ball roll past us like a hamster. Most—although not all—of the art was temporary, made to be enjoyed on "the Playa" (as we were learning to call the desert) and destroyed at the end of the Burn. Always, in the distance, we could see the Man himself, a forty-foot-tall sculpture waiting to be ritually sacrificed. The theme that year was "The Wheel of Time," and he was the center of the spiritual clockface around which the campsites were arranged, which was ironic, because I never saw an actual clock at the Burn—no watches either, or laptops, or pagers, or email, or cell phones. Date and day melted away, and were it not for the culminating burning of the Man, I think we all would have lost track of time permanently; lotus eaters living on sand.

"Wait up!"

We turned to see Stevie loping toward us, now clad in a shapeless muumuu. He was the most unprepossessing of the Mezbians, a collection of softnesses: soft brown eyes, soft white body, soft generous heart. We told him we were looking for the bone tree, and he fell into step with us.

"Look," he said, putting his arms around both of us, "we've all been talking, Ambra and I, I mean, and everyone else, and—what are your plans after this?"

Plans? No one talked about plans on the Playa!

"Well, after the bone tree I think . . . we'll come back to the tent?"

Stevie jumped in, a puppy unable to contain himself. "No, no, I mean, after the Burn?"

I'd been willing myself not to think about that. Though we had talked endlessly and aimlessly about buying a Westie—a kind of VW camper—and driving cross-country, in all likelihood, after Burning Man, Morgan and I would simply break up. Not wanting to admit that, we shrugged simultaneously, and Stevie broke into a huge grin.

"OK, so here's what—we were thinking—if you were into it—we, we want you to move to Seattle."

"What?" Morgan said, his nostrils flaring in disbelief. It never occurred to Morgan to try to hide what he was thinking, which was one of the things I loved about him. I always knew where he stood, even if I didn't always like it.

In a torrent of interlocking sentence fragments, Stevie explained: The Mezbians mostly lived in Seattle, where they were software engineers who made gobs of money. This was back when tech kids were still unabashed nerds, not Manosphere bros or would-be fascists (at least, not openly), and this made us trust them. They'd get Morgan a computer job, and until that point, they'd take care of us. (Like my father and myself, Stevie seemed to see no specific plan for *my* future, a troubling thought I decided not to dwell on.) We could ride back with them when the Burn ended, or if we *really* needed to go home first, Stevie had $5,000 on him—we could use that to fund our move, be there next week!

I was still trying to process the fact that Stevie had five large here just randomly, when he released us and bopped off into the distance. "Think about it!" he yelled over his shoulder. But Morgan had taken a bunch of acid earlier, and having a conversation about the future seemed like a real drag right now, so we continued walking.

Visions of our life in Seattle assembled in my head: Coffee. Grunge. Flannel. Tech. Starbucks. Nirvana. Morgan would do computer things, and I'd figure it out. As a New Yorker, I'd always viewed the West Coast with public disdain (it was so woo, and who liked constant sunshine anyways?), but that was a front masking my private curiosity. I'd experienced so little of the world—that was one thing Cornell *had* taught me—what did I know? I was so ignorant, I thought Seattle was sunny and San Francisco was warm!

Nothing felt real: not the desert, not the offer, not my future, not my past. But the mirage the Mezbians had planted in my head grew firmer with every step. Cornell didn't want me; why not take off? It had worked for coming to Burning Man. Here was the plan I'd been looking for. What more direct intersession did I need from the divine? I'd followed a sign to the desert, been wracked by trials, and found salvation. "Never let school get in the way of your education," Pigtailed Wendy had taught me, and wouldn't this be the best education—*life*?

"No," Morgan said flatly, his face trained on the glowing, swirling lights of the Triptonomicon, where we'd ended up after never finding the bone tree. I thought I'd been monologuing to myself this whole time, but in the deep recesses of Morgan's brain, he'd been processing.

"Bad idea," he told the Triptonomicon, words burbling up slowly. "Finish," he paused for a long time. "Then go."

I couldn't get any more out of him that evening, but I brought it up again the next morning, hoping he'd have a sober change of heart. Instead, we argued. When I pointed out that *he'd* dropped out and been fine, he snorted. He knew how to code, had gotten his GED, and was now receiving six-figure job offers. I was about to throw away three years of hard work for . . . what? What *was* I doing?

He sounded like my fucking father, and for the first time, I saw myself through Morgan's eyes. I didn't like it. I'd justified my erratic decisions because he was doing the same thing . . . except he wasn't. I was the one cutting school, daring them to kick me out because I was too much of a coward to make that jump myself. And I was doing the same with my parents. I was so worried about losing my tuition that it seemed I was intent on squandering it first. From a different angle, my radical adventure was just another tantrum by a privileged baby who'd been given the freedom to shit himself.

"Besides," Morgan went in for the kill, "aren't you doing the exact opposite of what that sign said? You're letting school decide what you do."

He was right, which I hated to admit, so I didn't, and it stuck in my craw for the entire fifty-four-hour bus ride back to Buffalo. Morgan left the Burn a day after I did, found Jeff wandering the streets of Reno, and had a crazy adventure that culminated with the pair of them getting arrested at a rest stop in Idaho; Morgan was let go, Jeff was institutionalized, and we never heard from him again. I got a C on my *Das Kapital* paper, but my professor asked if she could keep the duct tape envelope I'd made. My parents paid my tuition, or at least I assumed they had; we didn't talk about it, but I wasn't kicked out of school. Morgan and I did break up, amicably; he got his driver's license and bought a Westie, which he nicknamed "Smudge" after its oil leak. I have no idea what happened to the Mezbians, but I like to believe they found some other, more deserving wayward youths to take in.

I never went back to Burning Man, but I found sand in my hair, clothes, and bag for months afterward; sand in little corners of my room, sand in my sheets, sand everywhere, until it felt impossible that it had all come from the Playa, and I began to imagine it was slowly leaking out of me, like hope, like dust.

On the Line

I GOT MY FIRST CELL PHONE IN THE SUMMER OF 2000, right as I was graduating from Cornell, and hated it immediately. It was a dull gray brick with pink highlights around the buttons, a small antenna that pulled up from the side, and a tiny ASCII screen. Most of the time, it lived in the closet with the rest of my go bag: cash, change, a sealed water bottle, a variety of snacks, a first aid kit, and a two-piece set of XL women's pajamas. But two nights out of every week, I slept with it in my hand—although slept is really the wrong word; I lay in a torturous, half-awake state, willing the phone never to ring, jolted into panicked consciousness by every cicada or passing truck outside my window. My hotline shifts started at 4 p.m., when the Ithaca Rape Crisis Center closed, and ended at 9 a.m. when they reopened—a combined thirty-four hours a week of furious focus.

I didn't get any calls the first two weeks, which lulled me into a false sense of security, so on my fifth morning, I decided it was safe to take a shower before heading to work. After graduating a few months before, I'd bombed the GREs and took a gig working as the manager of Cornell's LGBT Center, where I'd been a student worker for years. It was a tentative step out of academia and into . . . something. I'd just sudsed up my hair—which was now so long it went past my waist when wet—when the buzzing began.

When a survivor called the line, they were connected with an answering service, who texted the volunteer on call—in this case, me—who then called the service back and was connected to the original caller. This way, I didn't have their direct number (ensuring their privacy), and they didn't have mine (ensuring that the whack jobs who used our hotline to jack off to rape fantasies couldn't call back after we hung up on them).

Wet, naked, and half-blind from the shampoo, I called the answering service. But it felt wrong to handle the call in the nude, so I fashioned my housemate's large, clean towel into a wrap dress with one hand (sorry, Jen), and dialed with the other.

"This is Ryan," I confirmed with the operator, who gave me the details: a social worker looking for resources for a client. I breathed a soapy sigh of relief for the layer of remove I had been granted for this, my first call. But the conversation was both harder and easier than I imagined: easier, because it turned out the social worker was actually looking for the Child Sexual Assault (CSA) hotline, not us; and harder, because in order to understand what she needed, I first had to hear the story of her client, a nine-year-old raped by her father.

Our center averaged only a few calls a day, mostly during business hours, so in order to afford a 24/7 emergency line, we shared it with two other antiviolence projects: the CSA line and what we then called the "Hotline for Battered Women." They were all community-created, feminist projects with their origins in the Seventies, a similar vein to the collective organizing that had created the Radical Faerie communes. I was the first "cis" guy to volunteer, though back then we just said guy, or usually I said nothing and let people around me make that call; right as I started, they also hired their first male staffer, who was there in part to expand services for LGBTQ survivors, though during my year on the line, every single call I received was from a cis woman assaulted by a cis man (except for the jackers, who hung up immediately when they heard my voice). Most of the callers just wanted to talk, but I accompanied women to the police station several times, and once to the hospital, which was why I had the go bag.

I'd started training for the line in the fall of 1999, shortly after I got home from Burning Man. It was another step away from academia, my now no-longer future. That it was also a number of other things—a coping mechanism; a sidestep toward therapy; a white-knuckled, last-ditch attempt to stop the screaming in my head—did not occur to me until many years later.

I've spent half a lifetime trying not to think about this.

The guy who tried to rape me was a tall, beefy chef, a real mountain of a man. We met in an America Online chat room;

yngm4m probably, or m4mwestchester. AOL had a lot of officially sanctioned chat rooms for boring straight people. Things got interesting in the unlisted rooms, which you could only join if you knew the room name. Many of these were gay (as were many of AOL's early users—an open secret in the tech industry of the time). I usually found them by adding "m4m" to the end of a place name or a vaguely sexual adjective. The big difference between this digital cruising and what had come before was a degree of permanency. Your chat name was your email address, and you had the option of creating a visible profile to go with it. Gay.com and Manhunt and GayRomeo and DudesNude and Adam4Adam and Grindr and Lex and Sniffies are all progeny of AOL, the original digital zaddy.

I thought that meeting men online was safer, because I could feel someone out and log off if they got weird. But not infrequently, I ended up sleeping with someone I'd have immediately avoided if we'd met in person. Very few of them were near me in age. Many of them hit on me constantly, an endless trickle of "sup?" or "a/s/l?" no matter how often I didn't respond. And then, of course, sometimes I did respond, on days when I was exceptionally horny or, more often, when I wanted something, *anything* to happen. I wasn't just looking for sex; I was looking to set time on fire, to transform empty evenings by applying a thin patina of sexual possibility. Mostly I did this when I was visiting my parents, for short weekends or occasional longer breaks forced on us by Cornell's calendar. I loved them, but I felt trapped when I was near them: uncomfortable in my skin, unable to sleep, always primed for an argument about how I was dressed or what I was doing with my life. Going online was my escape hatch, a way to leave my room without letting anyone in. I was always looking for *more*, and while the internet rarely provided it, it turned the dial of possibility from absolute zero to .001 percent. That it was just as likely to give me something I didn't want, and even more likely to give me absolutely nothing, didn't matter.

Or perhaps that was the point.

In Psych 101 we learned about an experiment in which pigeons pecked a lever to get a treat. Once they were trained, if the lever stopped working, they stopped pecking. If the lever continued working, they pecked whenever they were hungry. But if the lever worked inconsistently, occasionally giving a treat with no discernible pattern, the pigeons lost their minds, pecking the feckless lever endlessly.

I spent so much time worrying about being the pigeon, I didn't stop to think that, to someone else, I was the treat.

And also, the trick: Chef was one of the endless number of men online who offered me money for sex. Some were fun, some were aging but once hot, some were sad; some were foreign and thought American attitudes toward sex work were puritanical; some were famous and thought the world (and I) owed them; some were ugly and enjoyed paying to be told so. One had been nominated for an Emmy; one had produced a number of films I'd seen; one was a world-famous ceramicist, one, a would-be rapist, and one, a monster.

By the time I started saying yes to their offers—my junior year of college, years after they began—it seemed inevitable; this was what *people like me* did. Certainly in media, if anyone looked like me, they ended up a hooker, or dead, or a dead hooker—and it was "hooker," or "whore," or maybe "rent-boy" if they wanted to be demure about it; respectful terminology like "sex worker" was nowhere to be found in mainstream representation back then. From dramas like *Law & Order* to sitcoms like *All in the Family*, if queerly feminine people were on screen, they usually died, or were at least attacked for it, like Rickie in *My So-Called Life* (the first major gay teen on TV, whom I was obsessed with in 1994). This, I would later learn, was part of the long tail of the Hays Code, which censored film and TV production from the 1930s up until the 1970s and demanded that if gay characters appeared on screen, they did so as moral lessons on the dangers of homosexuality. But it wasn't just mainstream representations. In the fuck-you new queer fictions of Dennis Cooper and David Wojnarowicz, and in great indie queer films like *All over Me* and *Female Trouble* and *Twist* and *Paris Is Burning*, dolls and twinks were always depicted as sexual commodities in a violent underworld, and they usually came to a bad end. Drag queen or hooker (was there even a line between the two?): Those seemed like my available careers, and I'm no good at lip-syncing. Like AIDS, this was my inevitable future, so why not give in?

Plus, I liked sex, and I seemed good at it, and it was a far less degrading job than the slop line in the dining hall, where I spent a year dishing out endless portions to people who never looked me in the eyes. Sex and death were my lot in life, I figured, so I might as well get that money along the way.

(Once in a fight my mother yelled at me, "All anyone will ever see you as is gay," and I was furious, both that she thought that this was true *and* that she thought that this was bad. I didn't understand that we were trapped in different corners of the same matrix, both stuck reading the only script we'd been given about queer people. We were both convinced that death was riding my way on a pink horse. I thought I needed to change the world; she thought I needed to change direction. I hoped that things were getting better, but if I was wrong—if the world wasn't going to change—I refused to blink first, so I charged right back at death, as if we were high school boys playing gay chicken.)

All through junior year, I was working as a residential advisor to cover my housing, working at the LGBT Center after class, regularly being harassed on the street, always wondering if this was the day my parents would stop paying my tuition, slowly realizing that I'd spent years training for an academic career that was never going to happen. Sometimes all this made me angry, and sometimes it made me feel pathetic. Sometimes I looked down on the whole world, and sometimes I thought the entire world was looking down on me. Neither was true or healthy. I was always *pushing*, trying to make a long night last longer or a strange situation get stranger, to see what would happen next. I had many friends, but I kept them on the outside of my life and danced between groups so that I never had to go very deep. I was unhappy, but I also felt stuck, and so I drifted toward moments where things might break without my doing anything to make it happen. I made every stupid choice I made with my eyes open. Some part of me still thinks that's something to be proud of, and some part of me thinks that's the root of my problems right there: that desire to be special, no matter the cost.

Years later I approached sex work with a better attitude, as a job I was good at and enjoyed. (Shout out to those who remember Pete, the germaphobe with a classic six on Central Park West, who kept an entire generation of artists, actors, and would-be models afloat with his penchant for orchestrating real-life porn scenes that he could watch, fully dressed, from the safety of his mother's old armchair in the corner of one of the spare bedrooms.) But when I was twenty and twenty-one, it was often as much a form of self-harm as it was a cash cow.

I made bank, though, there's no denying that. What can a twenty-year-old do to make $300 an hour? Tell a guy he's sixteen.

Chef lived not far from my parents, and for about a year, I saw him every time I was home, maybe four times total. He paid in crisp hundreds, in white envelopes, in a way that said I wasn't his first. He was always asking to fuck me, the one thing I wouldn't do, because AIDS terrified me, I was mostly a top, and preparing to bottom was a lot of work. And I liked saying no to these guys; liked being a jerk about it too. It didn't matter if they were nice. I wasn't. At first I thought Chef was like the rest of them, guys who got off on having a young twink look down on them. But he was playing a longer game, and I was a dumb pigeon.

One night, we were just getting started, rolling around naked and hard when suddenly he was on top of me. He was 6'3", with probably 130 pounds on me, and I fit entirely under the outline of him. He was running his hands along my arms, moving me around like a puppet, which got uncomfortable after a minute, so I tried to pull my right arm down, only to find his thick left hand somehow encircling both my wrists, pinning them above my head. First I tried to slip one out, then the other; then I pulled, then I yanked, then I tried to roll over, but I was basically immobile—and then his other hand was pressing on my throat, and his knees were pushing my legs apart, and I went still because I knew then what was about to happen, and *this was what happened to people like me*. He saw me struggle, and he saw me stop, and he liked it. He laughed, a fake, funny, ha-ha laugh; a laugh that said when this was over, he'd act confused. We were having fun, weren't we?

Here's the truth: I could take being a whore; I could take being assaulted. In some weird way, this even felt like an initiation; this was what my life would be, and finally I was getting to it, awful as it was. What initiation comes without a bit of pain? But I have always been proud; too proud maybe. I can't take being dismissed. What a weird line to find in oneself.

When he laughed, I snapped.

He had to take most of his weight off me to guide his cock into me, and with just his arms holding my upper half to the bed, I curled onto the small of my back and kicked him with both feet, hard as I could in his chest. The first time shocked him; the second time knocked him off me. I bit his arm as he let go of my hands, hard enough that later I found blood on my sheets. Panting, we retreated to separate sides of the small room for a moment, and then *I* attacked *him*. Whatever scripts we'd been playing by had been discarded, and now he was scared of me, and I wasn't human anymore. I punched him in the stomach, and when he gagged and doubled over, I pushed him face down on the bed, fucked him hard as I could. Maybe that's where the blood came from. Afterward, he gave me the usual envelope and then $200 more. A bonus? A bribe? Was *he* scared of *me*? As soon as he was gone, the adrenaline flooded out, and the doubts flooded in. Had I misread everything? What if I was the monster in the room? *I* hit him; *I* fucked him; *I* took his money. I was an angry, unlovable thing stuck on the outskirts of gender. Good people didn't have rage issues. If I'd really been scared, I would have run the moment he was off me, or at least I wouldn't have remembered to use a condom. I made this happen. Consciously and unconsciously, I provoked people, my aunt was right, and what did I expect?

I blocked him online and never saw Chef again, and to this day, if anyone touches my throat when we're having sex, I'm back in that room trying to get him off me.

And yet, I think he saved my life.

Over my year on the line, I handled a dozen, perhaps fifteen calls total. Most were quite short, under twenty minutes, and although they were emotionally draining, they were also pretty easy. One woman had called regularly for years in moments of panic; we talked twice, about nothing, until she was able to catch her breath and make a plan for the rest of the day. Another called with very specific questions about the law but avoided any discussion of why or her own experiences. A third called because her sister had recently been raped, and she just needed to cry but didn't want to put that on her family or tell anyone her sister's business.

We started every call with the simple, most important question: Are you physically safe where you are right now? This was our guiding ethos: ensuring our callers were OK in the moment, then helping them plan what they wanted to happen next. In one way or another, all our callers had been violated, and we were there to help them take back control. Sometimes, just asking that question helped them see they were safe and calm down; other times, asking that question helped them see they were not safe at all, and we planned ways to get out.

The longest call I handled was six hours, but that was an exceptional circumstance. A young woman had made a report to the police about her attacker after hearing that he'd attacked someone else. But she was uncomfortable having him arrested, afraid that if she did, she'd end up the one on trial with the public, and nothing would happen to him. The police grew frustrated when she didn't return to press charges, so they picked her up during her shift as a waitress—nearly getting her fired—and held her in the station for hours. *Did she want this to happen to someone else?* they kept asking. Her friends called the hotline at her request, as the police wouldn't let her use the phone, and when I showed up, they wouldn't let me see her. *They've sent a man*, they told her. *Do you really want him to hear this?* I hated how easy it was to use the fact of my body against her, which was a constant worry I had while working the line, but eventually they let me bring her some food. Ithaca was a small town; turned out we knew each other socially. We talked for a while, and after a few calls to the police chief from the director of the crisis hotline, they let us leave. Despite everything the police did to her, she still did press charges, but she was right: Nothing happened to her attacker. Even when the police wanted to help, they were a blunt-force instrument that generally made things worse—a lesson that my years of research into the women's prison system would later confirm over and over again; a lesson I already knew from personal experience. The police are the only ones officially sanctioned to use violence and detain people against their will in our society, but those are cursed tools that taint their every use, until cops end up being the funhouse mirror image of the very violence they supposedly protect us against.

Sometimes I stayed on too long with the callers. We weren't trained therapists. We were meant to assist in a moment of crisis, then pass them on to someone who could really help. I was good at assessing their problems, listening, and responding to their needs, but when the time came to shuffle them off the line, I dawdled. It felt rude, or maybe evil? I had a constant bad feeling inside me those days, like I was always in the wrong, and I'd torture myself for ending the calls too soon—then do the same for letting them run too long.

My worst call was a little more than an hour. It started in the 5 a.m. twilight, and I watched the sunrise crawl across my bedroom floor as a woman in extreme distress told an urgent, tangled story about the man who raped her years ago; a senator's son, and now *they* were after her. Time and reality seemed to collapse for her as we spoke, or really, as she monologued, pausing only when a sob forced its way out of her. It was exactly the kind of call we weren't supposed to handle, and I fumbled it, letting her spin in paranoia because I knew that wild fear. It took me over for months after Chef. I saw nightmares everywhere, in everyone who stood too close to me. I was jumpy and weird when having sex, though I didn't stop. I still needed money, and men still offered it.

(I didn't need money. I *thought* I did. But my parents weren't going to stop paying my tuition; I just couldn't tell a real threat from the things we shouted while fighting. I didn't know any queer people with really supportive parents, and every bad thing seemed possible, or maybe like I deserved it. I would hold onto the money for a while, gripped by my fears, then waste it on clothes or presents for my friends. My bestie Tim would drive me to Syracuse and sing, "Gonna dress Hugh up in girl clothes," to the tune of Madonna while I shopped. Then something would set me off, and the cycle would start again.)

I was fine, I told myself adamantly, even as I moved all my bedding into the closet of my dorm room and slept there for months.

The last trick I turned—that time at least—was right around Christmas 1998, and it was so bad that afterward, I knew I needed to stop, even if I couldn't ask for help.

BobbyDee63 was a thirty-something loser whose AOL profile described him as having the body of a former baseball player, which stuck in my head because I had no idea what that meant (I still don't). I had a panic attack the second I got in his car. I was instinctually, illogically terrified. Thankfully he was one of those guys whose awkwardness over the situation made him chatty, and I let him babble about some other boy as he drove to his apartment.

By the time we arrived I had split in two: There was my body, a homunculus that I was piloting from very far away, and my mind, which was screaming on a loop. I remember him telling me his mother lived on the other side of the apartment and feeling immediately like it was a lie. His house was wildly messy. Not hoarder messy, exactly, but disordered in a way that was confusing. There were piles of things everywhere, but they felt haphazard, *wrong*, like why were his shirts hung on a bar directly above his bed? From the moment I walked in, I was convinced I was going to die there, at the hands of this pathetic schmuck who seemed like every townie who'd never gotten out of Westchester. But I also knew I was crazy, that nothing I was feeling had anything to do with the room I was in, and I had a fucking job to do (literally), so I did it.

Badly.

Turns out, it's hard to stay hard when you're terrified. Eventually, he asked me to piss in his mouth instead, and I couldn't even do that—no one had ever asked me before, and my bladder froze up. Everything else is jumbled. I don't think we had sex, or if we did, it wasn't for long. The next thing I really remember is getting dressed, the alarm still shrieking inside me. I turned to leave, and he was there, standing in front of the door, suddenly fully dressed in an entirely different, all-black outfit. I noticed then that he was much larger than me, built similarly to Chef: fat but strong. He was rooted in front of his door, like we were playing red rover, and he was going to stop me from coming over. But it was his face—his face had transformed, like when you're having a bad acid trip and you look in a mirror. He was an ancient evil wearing a sad suburban smirk.

When I met his eyes, I felt Chef's hands on my throat, and I knew that if I hesitated, I'd never leave that apartment. My skin felt hot and prickly, my body barely mine. I strode at the door as though he didn't exist, except our eyes were locked the entire way. At the last second, when I was about to push my way through him, he stepped aside.

I opened the door. We got into his car. We drove in silence. Maybe the radio was on, but we didn't say anything. He dropped me off where he picked me up, not far from my parent's house. It was late, dark, quiet, and nothing bad happened. I was just a broken, crazy faggot, projecting my fears onto anyone who came near me.

Months passed. I slept in my dorm closet. My application for the Truman fellowship was rejected. My friend Nic found me one night running a razor blade over my bicep, tracing thin, sticky red lines, for no reason I could explain other than it felt better than thinking. My grades slipped, and I never made dean's list again, but who cared—I knew by that point that I was done with school, and it with me. I headed down to work for the Progressive Party in DC, met Morgan, and tried to slip into his life.

Then, right before we headed to Burning Man, the police called.

About a month before we met, BobbyDee63 had raped and killed a twelve-year-old boy, leaving his body next to an abandoned ice-cream stand along the Saw Mill River Road. Eventually, I'd learn later, the police arrested nine men, a loose group of rapists, pedophiles, child pornographers, and, apparently, one murderer. If Chef hadn't come along a few months before,

I think I'd have hesitated when BobbyDee63 blocked his door, and who knows what would have happened next.

I cried quietly in my boss's office as the police spoke; it was the only phone I had access to that summer, other than the pay phones I worked.

I was different from the other kids the police had found on BobbyDee63's computer: older, a whore (I don't know if they knew that part, but I felt they could sense it on me). They were disgusted by me, and I was too. When I told them I couldn't remember very much about that night, they got angry. *How could I not remember? How often did I do this? What was wrong with me?*

I had all the same questions.

I didn't tell anyone about Chef or BobbyDee63. Not my family, not Morgan. The police never called again. I tried to go to a school counselor, but each time I started crying, couldn't stop, and just walked out. It felt like I had done something wrong, and I should be ashamed of it. It felt like nothing bad had happened, *really*, and I should be ashamed for acting like a baby about it. It felt like I drew every bad thing to me, and if I wasn't going to change, then I deserved what I got, and I had to learn to handle it. I never hated myself for being queer, but it felt like I had made a deal with the universe: If I wanted to live like this, this was what it would be.

And still—I took the deal, and would again in a heartbeat.

Besides, unless you were a blond virgin raped at gunpoint by a Black guy, sexual assault was barely considered a crime for anyone in those days. In 1998, the conservative paper on our campus published a "Dictionary of Cornell English," which defined date rape as the "most common form of interaction between male and female Cornellians" and the "term used by a woman the morning after a sexual act which she regrets." And that was for straight people. The only time queer sexual violence came up was in horrific "jokes" about dropping the soap in prison showers. When I hear people today talk about the #MeToo movement going "too far," I wonder if that's the happy time they'd like to return to.

Community hotlines like the one I worked came into existence because there was nowhere you could go and expect to be treated respectfully, let alone helped. But even at the rape crisis centers, there were few services for queer men—and not because we didn't need them. Even the government pushed the idea that guys couldn't be raped. Until 2012, the FBI Uniform Crime Report defined rape as "the carnal knowledge of a female, forcibly and against her will," leaving male survivors . . . nowhere. New York state's rape law wasn't expanded to cover nonvaginal penetration until 2024. A man could be sexually assaulted, but raped? No. Besides, weren't men supposed to want it all the time, *especially* gay men? Over the years, I've talked to so many friends my age about the sexual violence they endured in the '90s—violence they still to this day rarely call rape, or even assault. We were easy pickings: young, horny, taking risks with our bodies; illegally hanging out in bars because they were the only places to meet other queer people; eager to explore our sexual potential but afraid to talk to anyone about any kind of sex; without laws or family to protect us; and alone, so often alone.

I stayed on the hotline for about a year, and having to talk about sexual violence weekly cauterized the wound inside me. I didn't fully heal, but I stopped leaking. I decided to be someone else. I quit the line. I destroyed my cell phone. One morning, I woke up and asked a roommate to cut off all my hair. From now on, I'd be a cipher, unknowable and dangerous, with a different look every month. Slowly, I let go of everyone I knew, preparing for my next eleven years of constant moving. If anyone stepped to me again, I decided I'd hit first.

Burying the Twentieth Century

GIVEN ITS SLACKER IDENTITY, IT'S FITTING THAT THE Nineties drifted to an end well after it was technically supposed to be over. September 11 was the final nail in the coffin of the last millennium—well, four nails, 2,977 coffins. Two months prior I'd run pell-mell past airport security in San Francisco to catch a flight as guards cheered me on—an archetypal twentieth-century movie moment that would never happen again.

Our chickens had come home to roost, and in the aftermath we understood two things: that the world was becoming smaller every day and that being an American no longer protected us from the global shit we stirred. Connections and consequences: Those were the watchwords of our new era. Everyone got a cell phone. Traveling got more complicated and required more planning. You got obscurely nervous when you didn't hear back from someone quickly. Every police station declared some local landmark a terrorist target and was given wildly inappropriate military toys to protect it. Cameras appeared everywhere, and public spaces were fortified with gates, grates, and antihomeless architecture that made sitting anywhere uncomfortable. The analog empty days of my childhood were flaking away, and the disaffected aimlessness that Gen X had cultivated started to seem stupid, naive, dependent on citizenship in a global superpower where consequences didn't exist. We were born in the fuck-around century, but we were becoming adults in the find-out years.

So many things changed overnight after 9/11 that it took forever to understand we weren't just in some interstitial before normality resumed; we buried "normal" in mass graves in Manhattan, Afghanistan, and Iraq. Death, disruption, and more death: thus was the twenty-first century born.

I'd graduated Cornell the year before, but I was still living in Ithaca, spinning my wheels. I overslept that morning and woke up sometime between 8:46 and 9:03 a.m.; a housemate knocked on my door and told me to put on the radio just in time to hear about the second plane. He was unable to put any words to the tragedy that was unfolding—unlike my mother, who was articulate with rage when we spoke: *This is the British's fault!* she hissed, correctly. Were there other, more proximate causes? Yeah, sure. But my Irish American family can trace every global catastrophe back to the British Empire, and though the receipts might be longer than the ones at CVS, they're not wrong. She also told me that my cousin Matthew had to be evacuated from the American Express Tower next to ground zero—the windows on his floor had blown in; he was scratched up and scared but fine. All of our other relatives were accounted for, including my older brother Johnny, who worked in Union Square, and our father, who occasionally worked down at the Towers since he had retired from the IRS. Everyone I knew in the city was OK. *Thank God*, I thought on a loop, and *Fuck fuck fuck fuck fuck*.

At work, I opened the LGBT Center and made coffee as students drifted in unmoored from their class schedules, and then there were more students, and more coffee, and my boss brought food that no one ate, and then even more students came. Every seat in our one-room center was full, even the uncomfortable zebra-print novelty chairs shaped like giant stiletto heels. All of us had families in New York: strained, difficult, loving relationships that intruded into our thoughts, niggling us with fears of *what if what if what if*, and our thoughts were so loud, the room was quiet. If this had happened in 2011 instead of 2001, we'd all have been glued to Twitter, but without social media, we hewed together, hoping soon someone would get news from somewhere.

But the telephone lines were jammed, or maybe the world was ending; either way, no phones rang all morning until—out of nowhere—my cell phone buzzed around noon. My friend Sara was standing in a line down in the Financial District, because someone told her that at the front, the Red Cross was collecting blood, and it felt like doing something. Everything was covered in gray dust, she said, and smelled like burning plastic. She asked if I'd heard from our other friends—Brett, or Lauren, or Ari—and I realized I'd forgotten all of them the moment I heard my father was OK.

I was already drifting away from my life in Ithaca, even as I still lived there. In the coming weeks and months, I'd be horrified by American violence in the Middle East, terrified by the PATRIOT Act, and shocked by the nonsensical reactions of reactionary Republicans (*fucking "freedom fries," are you kidding me?*), but on 9/11 itself, nothing hit harder than the realization of the cliff edge I was perched on. If my parents had died that day, almost certainly our last interaction would have been a stupid fight, and in some internalized Catholic way, that idea felt as awful as if it had actually happened. Before the day was over, I told my boss I was moving back to New York City.

Back? That's how it felt, though I'd never lived there. I can remember my mother when I was younger—obviously having some bad day I didn't clock at the time—telling me urgently that I *lived* in the suburbs, but I was *from* New York City (spiritually if not, technically, literally). My parents might have left, but they would never unyoke our line from the city's lead. It simply isn't true that if you can make it there, you can make it anywhere; on the contrary, I think many of us could make it nowhere else, so thank God for New York City, that misfit archipelago with a concrete coastline.

But the realization of how much I had to lose did nothing to solve the issues that had made our relationship so fragile. We were in a five-year fight that flared up or went cold but never resolved or even paused; at most, it went unspoken—or we went without speaking, sometimes for weeks. That was easy to do back then, when you still had to worry about long-distance charges and making sure that everyone was within the cord length of a receiver when you called. Until very, very recently, being in constant contact was unusual, or impossible, or a sign that you were too high maintenance to hang.

Any time I did talk with my family, I steeled myself for an ambush. Thanksgiving of my freshman year, my aunt Eileen drove me back to Cornell. Our lives had always been closely entwined, ever since she and her son Christian moved in with us when I was four. She was the earthiest of my mother's sisters: loving, raunchy, bullshit-less, and prone to saying the things other people only thought. On the drive, we listened to Howard Stern until the radio cut out, then moved on to a series of motivational tapes. Eileen's softly curled hair jiggled in the wind as she chain-smoked the Parliaments that every woman in my family carried in her purse—a sure sign that she was Thinking about Something, capital *T*, capital *S*.

An hour outside Ithaca, she abruptly ejected the cassette, and the screech of the magnetic tape slamming to a stop felt like a warning. She launched straight into a conversation she'd been having in her head for hours.

"What if," she said, "you just get a girl pregnant?"

This was an unhinged opening gambit, made all the worse because I was unsure of the direction of the question: suggestion or rhetorical warning? I didn't know if she knew I was gay. Aside from the therapist, my parents told me to tell no one. But because my family is close-knit and gossipy, *they* told other family members seemingly at random, who—sworn to secrecy—immediately told *just* their sisters or mothers or closest cousins. I was living in a glass closet, and every time I was around my family, I could feel their knowing eyes on me, or at least thought I could.

"We'd take the baby," Eileen continued. "We could raise it until you graduate. And you could just come out and break up with her!"

So: suggestion it was.

What problem she thought she was solving, I wasn't sure. Since I had come out to none of my relatives directly, I had no gauge by which to tell what they were thinking. "Mmhmmm," I murmured a few times, perfectly blank, doll-like with embarrassment, until she turned the tape back on, and Deepak Chopra rescued me with some deep breathing.

What was there to say? Often in those years, the calm and respectable thoughts of the straight world—even those of the people in it who loved me deeply, like Aunt Eileen—seemed insane to me, and I had no idea how to engage with them. If I opened my mouth, I was pretty sure I'd eventually start screaming. Avoidance was the easiest answer.

The longer I was in college, the less I came home. The more I pulled away from my family, the more panicked they became. Before every vacation, we fought about how long I'd be home for, ensuring that no matter how short my stay was, it felt far too long.

I was not alone in this dance. On holiday breaks, Cornell's campus became a ghost town inhabited mostly by foreign students, poor kids, and queers. Every self-respecting gay bar back then had free community events on Thanksgiving and Christmas, because holidays and homecomings were such fraught ground. I think most straight people—including my parents—thought of queerness as lonely because all they saw of *our* lives were the boundaries that kept us out of *their* lives.

That too was changing. In the new millennium, straight people were learning about queer people just as much as Americans were learning about Iraqis. It was stupid *Will & Grace* shit. A sitcom-level understanding—knowledge that was partial, filtered, bias soaked, and unreliable. But it replaced the nothing that had been there before. We analog children—Xennials, as I supposed we're called now—spanned this gap, both in the world and in our personal lives. We were the bridge between the centuries, between analog and digital, between the old world, where we knew nothing, and the new one that overwhelmed us with too much information at all times.

In 1997 (a few months after my drive with Eileen), I went back to my high school to talk to student leaders about growing up queer in our small town. I was nervous and nineteen and full of declarative slogans: Silence equals death! Gay is good! Ethical slut! ACT UP fight AIDS! I wanted to be provocative, to hide the fact that I was nervous. As the forty-five minutes of class ticked down, I sped up, saying more words with less meaning. I had an outline, but I left it behind because I wanted to seem prepared. When we got to the Q&A, one of the student leaders immediately raised her hand. I knew her, a little: She was one of the many students who attended a strict Korean Christian church nearby. What can *we* do? she asked—the essential element I'd completely forgotten.

Together, we made a list of possibilities, most of which were pretty anodyne: Don't use words like *dyke* or *fag*; don't assume everyone is straight; use your status as student leaders to set the tone, etc. Small potatoes from today's vantage point, but I knew from experience just how groundbreaking those ideas were in Irvington, New York, at the time. When I was a high school senior, I'd done a survey on attitudes toward gay people in our school, and the responses had been nightmarish. More than one student wrote that if a sibling came out, they'd kill them, and if a teacher came out, they'd get them fired. It felt revolutionary just to use the word *gay* as something other than an insult, and while some of the students gawked at me like a sideshow—I doubt they'd ever met an out gay person—they took our talk seriously.

But nothing comes without consequences.

I rode the high from that high school presentation for exactly four days, before word got back to my parents. My cousin was the guidance counselor for crissake—how did I not realize that was going to happen? On some level, I must have wanted it to. Have you ever watched a cat nudge a glass toward the edge of a table, the way they love to see how close they can get before it falls? That was me in those days, smashing glasses and running away.

I was back in my dorm room at Cornell—a fifth-floor turret in a castle-like building plopped down next to the gorge that divided North Campus from Central—when my mom called. We launched straight into a fight. I don't remember where we started, but eventually my mother screamed, "Jim is going to be harassed because you're gay. This is your fault."

The last thing I said before I slammed the phone down—and these were old, heavy, Bakelite institutional phones, so you could really smash that receiver—was that Jim was going to be harassed because *he* was gay, and at least I was doing something about it, while they were just getting in the way.

Was I right? Absolutely. My brother Jim and I were so similar, it was easy to see that he was following in my fancy little footsteps. Did saying so help him? Absolutely not. It did, however, hurt my mother, which was my real goal.

(In a sideways way though, my mother was right too. As more of us came out, we became increasingly visible—sometimes *because* we were out, but just as often because people now knew what to look for. In every sense, as we took up more of the public world, we had less private to retreat to, and that was true even for young people who had made no conscious decision to come out. Connections and consequences: That was the new millennium.)

One rare night when I was home, my mother—well in her cups—told me that I had made myself ugly, by which she meant gay, by which she meant femme, by which she meant trans, by which she meant weird, by which she meant a stranger to our family, the fundamental unit of our existence. Gut struck and furious, I called her a jealous bitch who'd always been ugly. Thank God, before either of us could swing again, my father pulled my mother from the room, saying if we kept this up, we'd come to hate each other, and he wasn't going to stick around for that.

Attack, retreat, retrench, revenge—we spun in the same circle every time we saw each other, until it was too much, and I flung myself away again.

Jim was entering middle school, and I often think that if I'd been better, if I'd known how to talk about my feelings, I could have been there for him during that, the worst period in every gay person's life. Instead, I was fighting with our parents. But it was so much easier to scream at someone else for being wrong than it was to figure out what was right.

Or at least, it was until September 12, 2001.

By October, I'd found someone to take over the lease on my room in Ithaca, and by Christmas I was parked temporarily in my parents' basement, responding to Craigslist ads for roommates and printing out MapQuest directions to somewhere called . . . *Brooklyn?*

Before I found anything I could afford, however, a new, more personal series of tragedies struck, starting with the death of my cousin Damian. He had just been released from prison and was on his way to pick up his son when he met up with some old friends, shot up, had a bad reaction, and was left to die in the elevator shaft of an abandoned building in Yonkers. My whole life, I'd been part of a cohort of thirty first cousins who got together in a raucous and mixed-match assembly many times a year: Christmas, of course, and Easter and Thanksgiving; if there was a wedding or a particularly momentous anniversary; perhaps a christening, or birthday, or retirement party, or that time my cousin Christian got a short film accepted to the Yonkers Film Festival, and we all rented a yellow school bus and piled in like a frat party on wheels. Damian had missed many occasions—prison'll disappear you like that—but then again, so had I, and the cousin-Borg absorbed us both back every time we returned. Like so much else, that wholeness was now just a twentieth-century memory.

Before Damian's death, for the first few weeks I'd been home, my parents and I tiptoed around each other in their big, old, now mostly empty house. Anytime I found myself alone with them, I sidled out quickly, like a feral cat, the hair on the back of my neck all prickled up. They were pleased and unclear as to why I was there, and I couldn't bring myself to say the simple truth, that I loved them and was scared of losing them. It *was* true, but it was entangled with an equally powerful, much more difficult truth: that I was still angry, and even if I had a dim glimmer of all the ways *I'd* been shitty over the past few years and how much *I* stood to lose, my pride would not let me bow my head. If I dwelled too much on our history, an angry voice began whispering, *If they cared so much about Jim being harassed because I was gay, why didn't anyone care what was happening to me?* No matter how much I wanted to be on the other side of our fighting, some part of my soul insisted, *They started this; they have to end it.*

(This was a truth I could not put into words then but would learn later as a writer: Whether on a global scale or a personal one, the morality of every story depends on where the story begins. For many Americans, 9/11 felt like the beginning of a new era of global aggression *against* us, but that story only made sense if you ignored the decades of our aggression that preceded that day.)

Could I love my parents without saying it? Could I love them without forgiving them? I tried, for those first few weeks. I tried, but it was an exercise in self-abnegation, pretending to feel anything but what I felt, and the longer we existed like that, the more it seemed like our inevitable future: a negative peace, without forgiveness or expiation.

I tried, and then death came for a second lick of the ice-cream cone: The night after Damian's funeral, my father's mother died. Two years earlier, her daughter—my closeted butch lesbian aunt Alice—had died a slow, bad death from kidney cancer, and ever since my grandmother had been in deep dementia, which had revealed or created a scared and angry side to her—especially when it came to my mother, whom she would only refer to as "that woman." As in "*That woman* hates me" and "If I eat too much, *that woman* is going to put me out on the streets." As a result, grandma wouldn't eat much other than cookies, which she hid in her pockets and then forgot, until she left a trail of stale crumbs everywhere she went. It must have been excruciating for my parents to live with her—something I didn't think much about while I was away. She was a ghost wearing the ruined and most toxic form of someone they loved. She was their past erased and their future made manifest nightmare. Finally, when the live-in nurse could no longer care for her, they moved her to a home not far away, and we all knew when they called around midnight what it meant.

Death, disruption, and more death: Thus was my adulthood born. I think that's how all adults emerge, through those moments when the cocoon falls away and whatever you are is exposed. When I was a child and someone died, it was simple, straightforward, and purely sad, a natural consequence of being old (by which I meant over thirty). With Damian and my grandmother, there was a thin, excruciating lining of relief. The terrible call had come, and it could never come again. But that relief was a direct conduit to guilt, and it surged around us, asking, *What if what if what if.* Whom had we failed, and whom were we still failing? What other new disasters would this century bring?

The immediate aftermath of the nursing home's midnight call was messy. We hosted another wake and funeral at our house, running on the fumes of the first, this time mostly for my father's family, an entirely different—yet equally large—sprawl of Irish American New York City Catholics. Clean the house, pick the dress, arrange the viewing, announce the wake—and who would handle the catering, and write the obituary, and did anyone have cousin Larry's number? No, Larry *Brady* not Larry *Ryan*.

A numbness, a get-it-doneness settled in on all of us, and we slipped into our oldest, easiest roles: hosts. If there was one thing we knew how to do, it was throw a party—even if it was a funeral.

For days, we moved like Victorian automatons, each well oiled on our busy track, running in perfect parallel until finally, somehow, it was over, and the house was empty again, and I found myself sitting with my mother on the threadbare pink love seat that had been her mother's, which sat uncomfortably in our formal living room that was reserved for Irish relatives and visiting priests.

"I'm sorry," my mother said suddenly, looking straight ahead at the now quiet room filled with furniture we'd soon give away. I froze, wary of any intensities between us, which always seemed to spiral into a fight. "I'm sorry," she repeated firmly, her head shaking, the rest of the sentence trapped, tears running silently down her face. "We were so awful"—her voice broke, tearing the word *awful* in two, shoving a sob between its syllables, so it sounded like she was full of wracking awe—"when you came out . . . we just . . . didn't know any better."

It had never occurred to me until that moment that the fear I felt on 9/11 was a shadow of the fear they carried every day: that someone would kill me for who I was, and they wouldn't have been able to stop it, and our last interaction would have been some stupid motherfucking fight.

I started crying then, shaking, saying, "I'm sorry I'm sorry I'm sorry," and we hugged, awkwardly sideways but still desperately clinging to each other.

After a while, we stopped crying. Stopped hugging. Sat. Said nothing. The slippery protective plastic squeaked beneath us as we wiped our eyes and drew shallow breaths. And for the first time in many years, I was not uncomfortable in her presence.

We sat like that for a long while, and by the time we stood up, the old world had been buried, and we took our first slow steps into the new.

The Center Cannot Hold

KENDALL WAS A GOOD KID, DESPITE ALL THE LITTLE LIES. He wasn't born in Australia, or scouted by a modeling agency, or the son of rich and loving parents. His name wasn't even Kendall, but who cared? Our after-school drop-in program for queer youth saw about a hundred kids a day, ages thirteen to twenty-one, and if he wanted to leave his real life behind when he walked in, well, there was probably a good reason. Our administration billed us as an educational enrichment program for LGBTQ+ youth, but in truth we were a social service agency for queer kids in desperate need, many of them homeless or unsafely housed. As one of the staff therapists explained when I was hired, the question wasn't really *if* our youth had been abused; it was *when* and *by whom* and *for how long*.

God, in my mind now Kendall looks so young: pimply faced, dark-skinned, light eyed, hair at first long and awkward—too curly for that flat middle part that ruled the '90s—then short and spiky with bleached tips. We played *Magic: The Gathering* on slow days, and he smoked me. His look was boy band but his attitude was goth; he loved comic books; he was quiet but a total smart-ass; and his only close friend was Dubois, a little punk who wore neo-Nazi band patches because he thought it would stop people from beating his ass. Dubois had the kitty, and it showed: so skinny, no meds, no home. We had to kick him out too, after he started spitting blood at people. But Kendall was long gone by that point.

I was maybe seven years older than him, tops. "Coño," Deb said the day she hired me, "how are we gonna tell you from the kids?"

But it was easy; I was the White guy who spoke only basic Spanish in a room that was 95 percent people of color, 60 percent bilingual.

It was as far away from Cornell as I could get; still, Cornell got me in the door. At my first interview, the assistant director said he'd noticed my résumé because he'd gone there as well. My degree was a chit that held currency anywhere, everywhere—except at the drop-in center, where the students didn't know Cornell and wouldn't have cared if they did. I was hired to be part of a sea change that never fully happened (thank God), but Kendall and the other kids got caught up in it anyway, and for that I'm sorry.

Our center was rocketing down the same trajectory as many queer nonprofits in those days. We were launched in the '70s by post-Stonewall grassroots activists who worked out of their homes to provide desperately needed services to a newly visible community that was so stigmatized, they could rarely go anywhere else. In the 1980s, the urgency of AIDS turbocharged both the need and the funding for the center, allowing it to grow and secure a permanent home, even as many of its founders passed away from the crisis. As more people came out and the straight world began to take AIDS seriously in the '90s, our center was able to access more government and foundation money.

But this moment created a fork in the path. As the stigma against gay people began to (slowly, unevenly) recede, those with the most social capital—rich, White, cis, male, US born, with health care, nonaddicted, etc.—began to pull away from the service side of the movement. The work of grassroots activists combating homophobia meant these people could now get their needs (social, educational, medical, etc.) met from places that were not gay specific. They began to be credentialed by important straight organizations, and those credentials soon came to be seen as more important than years of activism or community ties in selecting the leadership of these nonprofits.

The people receiving services, meanwhile, were increasingly people for whom homophobia and transphobia were among a panoply of issues they were facing. As AIDS became less of an organizing center for the queer community, gay money began to move in new directions—specifically, toward the campaign for gay marriage, which took off in the early 2000s. Marriage was billed as a straightforward issue of discrimination, which, of course, it was, but it was also an issue that largely concerned people who owned property, worried about inheritance, had employer-provided insurance, were able to be out, etc. What did a campaign for gay marriage do? It allowed us to live more like straight people, without asking fundamental questions: Was marriage itself a good system or one that would do much to help the queer community? Love wins, sure, but *United States v. Windsor*, the 2013 Supreme Court case that opened the door for same-sex marriage to be legalized, was brought by Edie Windsor to avoid having to pay $300,000+ in inheritance taxes when her partner died.

Queer nonprofits like ours had grown out of a bottom-up mentality, helping those with the most needs, because the stigmas against gay people were so widespread, it was easy to imagine even the richest, Whitest, cis-est homo in the world ending up abandoned and in need. When respectability was not an option, respectability politics carried little weight in the queer world. Marriage was not generally a priority in those years. But around the time I started working at our center, the paradigm flipped, and the funding focus increasingly became the needs of those at the top of the social hierarchy: people whose only challenges were homophobia and transphobia; people like the imaginary youth our center *wanted* to serve rather than those who actually walked through our doors.

After more than twenty years as a renegade social service agency, half in and half out of New York City's government, our center was left reeling: serving a population with increasing needs, right as queer money moved away and straight money moved in—with a lot of baggage in tow.

Every grant came with new regulations to follow, and every major donor wanted a tour of the drop-in center, complete with squeaky-clean kids prepped to stroke their egos. Without that influx of cash, our center might well have closed before Kendall ever arrived. When I started, there were still weeks when managers were told not to cash their paychecks immediately, or they'd bounce. My starting salary was $25,000, with minimal benefits. We were in trouble, and money was necessary to fix some of those problems. But once the money came, we were beholden to it, and our new first priority was to keep it flowing. The money made more of everything: more staff, more computers, more supplies, more rules . . . well, more of everything except kids. The money made our space *safer*, partly by pushing away the youth who had the most needs.

Like Kendall.

Everywhere, the walls between queer and straight life were falling, but it was hard to tell which had been protecting and which constraining us. I started working at the center in early 2002, which (turns out) was the year that gay bars started to disappear, and today—despite all our social advances and the rainbow onslaught of corporate pride every June—fewer than 50 percent survive. Most of the places I went to back then are gone now: Tunnel, Roxy, Limelight, Escuelita, Meow Mix, Flamingo East, Cattyshack, The Starlight Lounge, ToyBox, Urge, The Hole, Excelsior, Splash, Easternbloc, Bum Bum Bar, I C Guys . . . all gone. And the gay bookstores too, and the gay travel companies, and most of the bathhouses, the gay real estate places, gay funeral homes, gay newspapers; the whole parallel pink world couldn't survive the harsh light of acceptance. Yes, those spaces were often racist, misogynist, ableist, and just plain tacky. And I can't deny we got so much in return for giving them up. My younger queer cousins today live lives that were unimaginable when I was their age. Queer people now are all the places we weren't when I was a kid: on TV, in my hometown, in schools. But we sacrificed many of our private spaces for our share of the commons, and there are nights when I feel unfit for this new world, a relic of the shadow times, uncomfortable with public affection, disinterested in bars with straight people—an old puppy who longs for the safety of his crate.

Really though, I stopped going to most bars when I started working at the center. I couldn't take the static of finding my students in places they shouldn't be, like the time I caught Kendall and a pair of fifteen-year-olds trying to sneak into a sex party a friend was throwing. I struck all of Christopher Street off my mental map of the city the day I met some friends there for an early breakfast and saw Kimmi coming off the stroll, her wig all fucked up and her skirt so short it could have been a belt. We chatted inanely about school for a bit, and I told her to come see me on Monday, but she didn't show up all week, and I got paranoid that she was dead and I'd been the last one to see her and had done nothing—a stupid savior fantasy passed through a worrywart filter. After that, for a few years, I avoided most gay places in the city.

Besides, we had a queer world all our own. I'd seen *Paris Is Burning* in college, but I didn't really know that scene until I started working at the center. I learned quickly that "ballroom" was the competition that grew up around "voguing," an art form / battle mechanic created by incarcerated queer folks of color in New York City's infamous prison, Rikers Island, in the 1970s. "Houses" were a cross between competing voguing teams and chosen ballroom families, a source of both support and recognition for people who were rarely given either.

At our center, we had voguing icons on staff and up-and-coming legends among the youth. Luna Khan taught me to serve face, Tyhierry Mizrahi showed me how to duck walk, and the one time we threw our own ball, Octavia St. Laurent herself (*The* Heavenly Angel) gave me my tens. My students taught me that "cunt" was the highest compliment one could give, "fierce" was now an insult, and that depending on the circumstance, a tongue pop could be a withering clapback, a minor compliment, or just the verbal equivalent of an exclamation point at the end of a sentence. They taught me there was a queer, Black, Latiné scene where the functions in rented halls in Bed-Stuy and Harlem never started before 2 a.m., no matter what the flyer said. They taught me about LaBeija (the first house), and 007s (those walking a ball without yet being in a house), and how the commentator's flow both directed the competition and riffed on the beat.

Our ballroom kids were the first people I met for whom gender seemed truly to exist on a spectrum. It was right there, in the language they'd created. In the outside world, *trans woman* and *gay man* were in opposition, far quadrants on a poorly understood four-square grid. But their ballroom equivalents, *femme queen* and *butch queen*, were connected intimately, etymologically. Like the queen of diamonds and the queen of spades, they were different suits of the same card, different expressions of a shared essence.

For the first time, I encountered a language—a logic—that captured (in a positive light) the truth that shitty kids had grasped intuitively in the '90s: that queer gender and queer sexuality were not fully separable, not for all of us at least. The majority of my femme queen students had always known they were women and were doing the hard work of bringing their lives and bodies in line with that knowledge. But there was always a solid minority of youth whose gender journeys were looser, without a set end point, or recursive, doubling back on themselves and back again until they knit identity into the fit they needed. For some, this was a painful process, equal parts self-discovery and self-doubt. For others, it seemed as natural as breathing, and no matter what bullshit the world tossed at them, they followed an inner sense of self that wasn't tethered to the rules of sexual identity defined by straight people in the late 1800s. They taught me that an experience did not have to be unchanging or permanent to be real; that *ser* and *estar* are both ways to be.

One week, we got a massive donation from Henri Bendel, the luxury department store. All the clothes were more than a year and a season old, making them unsellable trash in the eyes of the 1 percent who could afford them. We brought in a pack of Fashion Institute of Technology grads to transform our cafeteria into a makeshift boutique, and each student got to choose five pieces of clothing. But contractually, we had to destroy any evidence of where the clothes came from to prevent students from reselling them, so staff spent the morning pulling $1,000 tags off ostrich leather miniskirts. Freed from the frivolous valuation of the outside world, our students immediately attacked the clothes they picked with scissors, bleach, and markers, breaking and remaking them into something that fit them better. For the next month, all our femme queens looked like rich bitch supermodels.

I didn't realize I was seeing the future, but where else would it come from? The world said they were so marginal they didn't matter, but being so far outside the mainstream meant that everything our students created was new, even the genders. Let stolid adults chase marriage; our youth wanted spaces where they could become more themselves, not more like the straight world that continually fucked them over (because of their sexuality and gender, of course, but also their color, their bank balance, their accent, etc.). In little pockets all over the globe (and the internet), young people were reimagining what it meant to be queer, and it was a blessing to hold the space in which they did it. Boomers and Gen Xers wrote the theory; Millennials and rising Zoomers lived it. We called the corners; they summoned the new world.

It healed me to cheerlead those journeys—no, that's not quite right. In order to support those journeys, *in order to do my damn job*, I had to heal. Because how could I love in my students what I hated in myself? I adopted a new motto in those years, a line stolen from the band Everything but the Girl: Never have the same face twice. My queerness—my queen-ness—didn't exist in being femme or butch; it was in the variability itself. Every day I felt less defined by my body and therefore more able to enjoy it. For a few years, I existed almost entirely in a queer world, and the constant worry of having to be sensible to straight sensibilities faded (except when I had to fill out grant reports).

Is it any wonder I miss those shadows? In that nourishing darkness, I learned to see myself more clearly.

Officially, Kendall hated ballroom. He complained about the way the kiki kids took over the boom box every afternoon, playing "The Ha" on loop while they practiced their duck walks and dips. But even he screamed and snapped when Leiomy took the floor. She was undeniable, even back then, long before *America's Best Dance Crew* and *Legendary* made her TV famous. Once I saw her and Barry stack two metal desks, climb on top, and leap almost to the ceiling before they slammed their bodies to the ground in death drops that shook the world. And with Dede commentating? It was pure fire, five days a week—though every once in a while, all that energy made the room explode.

That was our biggest problem, at first: Most afternoons we had a hundred kids, one room, and just me and Juli to keep the peace. That day, that terrible day, the day I quit in my heart, it was so hot, and Kendall and Manny kept reading each other—well, Manny read Kendall, and Kendall tried to keep up. Separating them didn't help; they just sniped each other by the bathrooms and in the line for dinner. We thought it was squashed by the time we shut down for the night, but trudging through the thick heat on my way to the F station at Second Avenue, I saw the commotion outside McDonalds and knew my night was fucked. Not once, in the two and a half years I worked at the center, was I ever really off the clock.

Inside it was fast-food pandemonium: everyone yelling, food all over the floor, a loose circle of kids howling, "Fuck him up!" Kendall was little and quick; Manny was slow, femme, and big, standing rooted like a kung fu panda while Kendall darted, at him and back, at him and back, trying to slap Manny's face without getting grabbed.

Although the center's new admin expected us to stop fights, they refused to train us on de-escalation methods, because that would mean admitting the kids could be violent, which went against the image they were projecting to our funders of "good" kids whose only problem was a homophobic school or family. In the mirror of these imaginary students, our funders saw themselves and opened their wallets. But our work then had to be reorganized around these faux priorities to keep the money flowing, and de-escalation training was not on the list. So when fights (inevitably) broke out, we did the only thing we could and stepped between our students. Not once did I ever see a youth hit a staff person.

Not on purpose anyway.

As soon as Kendall recognized my face, he stopped moving. Manny dropped his hands. I said, "Cool it," as though we were in a community production of *West Side Story*. The other kids started making that rising *Ooooooo* sound that means someone's in trouble, and I thought it was over. But then Manny rushed past me, checking Kendall hard with his shoulder, sending him flying. Most of the kids took off after him as I helped Kendall up, and next thing I knew, I was racing after Kendall, racing after the trail of kids, racing after Manny, all the way up to the K-Mart on Astor Place that everybody said was the death of the neighborhood. Kendall slammed through the glass doors screaming, “Imma kill you, you fat fuck,” and that’s when he pulled the knife.

It wasn’t even a big knife. Not like the honkin’ huge steak knife that Peaches always carried in her purse or the Crocodile Dundee bowie knife that “straight” hustler showed up with one day. It was a pocket switchblade, the knife part itself maybe three inches long.

Unofficially? The floor staff knew a lot of our kids carried knives, or shivs, or mace. Their lives were dangerous. But so long as we never saw them, we didn’t have to confiscate them. Back in the day, we asked students to check their weapons with the guard at the door, to keep our space a sanctuary, but under the new regulations, that was verboten: If something happened, and we were sued, that would be evidence of our knowing negligence. Our ignorance wouldn’t protect the kids, but it would protect the institution. Even marginal queer spaces, like ours, were being constrained by the bounds of a kind of propriety. The more money and recognition we received, the more rules and regulations we lived by. Our administration wanted to ensure that every youth we served was a success (on paper at least), and they were just as willing to ban “underperforming” youth as they were to expand services for the rest.

And it wasn’t just us. For decades, the decaying industrial pier at the end of Christopher Street had been a gathering place for working-class gay men, trans women, and those who partook of both identities. As the neighborhood became less of a “gay ghetto,” the city decided to fix up the piers. The first step? Fencing them off for years, leaving the queer youth of color who’d claimed them with nowhere to go. I joined Community Board 2 and tried to negotiate something for our kids—gender-neutral bathrooms during construction, a promise that the new piers would have dedicated space for queer youth, fucking *anything* in return for what they were taking, that shitty little bit of turf that was all my kids could count on. But the consensus was that the new park would help the neighborhood, where gay people owned property after all, and if our kids didn't fit in, it wouldn't be because they were gay—it would be because they were bad. It was the same message they received everywhere else, and I knew what it was like to internalize the idea that you were every fucked-up thing they said you were. If I were Kendall, I'd have carried a knife too.

Right inside the K-Mart doors, I managed to grab Kendall's empty arm and yank it, so we both slammed into the wall, and I braced myself against him as he yelled, "Imma fuck you up! Imma kill you!" and waved his knife over my shoulder at Manny, who finally realized he'd pushed Kendall too far and fled down the steps to the basement exit that led straight into the subway.

Kendall wanted me to stop him, that was obvious. He could have fought harder, slipped from my grasp—hell, if he'd poked me with that knife, I'd have let him go. Kendall didn't want to kill Manny; he wanted to scare him, the way *he* was scared, the way so many of us, back then, were always scared. What little safety we had to offer ended right outside our doors. Sakia Gunn used to come to our center, before she was stabbed to death on her way back to Jersey one night in 2003, and it was us the police called to identify Mari's body when they were found dead in the Gowanus Canal in 2004. One year, on the first day of school, a clan of homophobic whack jobs showed up across the street waving signs that said, "GOD HATES FAGS." My parents and younger brother Jim joined the hundreds of counterprotestors that morning, chanting, "Two four six eight / we see your hair / it's you God hates." It was a salve on my soul to see their faces in the crowd. And by the time the bell rang to start our day, so much press had arrived that our kids treated the sidewalk like a red carpet, sashaying past the cameras until the protesters nearly had a coronary! *That* was a good day.

But mostly the violence was routine and banal, like the time Kendall showed up trying to hide a black eye and just shrugged when I asked where he got it. None of this is an excuse for what Kendall tried to do to Manny, but how could we expect our kids not to reach for violence when violence was constantly reaching for them?

That's what I tried to explain to management the next morning, but it didn't matter. We were visible now, and public disorder required public punishment. Kendall was banned from our center. I never even got to say goodbye.

"You can't save people," my mother sighed one afternoon. We had started meeting to explore the flea markets that took over empty Manhattan parking garages on the weekends back then, before they were all turned into condos. It felt, oddly, like making a new friend as an adult: both of us a little shy but putting in the time. "It's not just *not* your job," she said, as we picked through chipped art deco knickknacks. "It's not possible. You help them where they are." She had spent decades working with autistic kids. It was a world away, but the struggle was the same: how to show up every day and do your best, knowing full well your best would not be enough. We weren't saviors; we were care workers. Kendall was gone; the work continued.

But it never felt right again.

A suspicion crept in among those of us who worked the after-school program: This was what the administration wanted. Fewer "high-risk" kids. More kids who could provide the "outcomes" and "metrics" that win major government contracts. They wanted *Glee*, but we were much closer to *Euphoria*.

They couldn't just kick kids out—that would have been immoral, and worse, obvious. But they could twist every part of our work, until coming to our center required jumping through so many hoops, the kids with the most needs just couldn't keep up. They reduced our hours, stopped serving dinner, hired White guys with Ivy League degrees who didn't speak Spanish, and nixed the supportive service staff, the food pantry, and the free clothing and toiletries we used to give out like candy on Halloween. Our long-term educational staff was replaced by city-vetted experts, who were all out of their depth, and when that led to a series of student-teacher clashes, a wave of young people were kicked out. We were told that youth with criminal records were most likely "inappropriate for services," as were youth who dressed too sexually or cursed too much. Finally, they declared an end to our drop-in program entirely. No longer was it enough to keep kids safe and fed; now, every youth had to be in a structured lesson at all times. We were being watched more closely than ever, so we watched the kids more closely too—an early foretelling of our new world of constant surveillance. But since we had so few staff, this meant we put a cap on the number of youth we let in every day, and the ones who couldn't sit in a circle and discuss their feelings, or quietly do an art workshop, or participate in after-school tutoring? Bounced. All of them.

You know what shocked me though? The other social service organizations—the straight ones, the ones our students usually tried first before they filtered their way to us—stepped up. They saw the sudden influx of queer kids in need, kids *we* were turning away, and they built incredible programs for them. As tentative as I can be about this new world, I know that would never have happened in the shadow times. For as much as we could no longer flout their rules, they could no longer ignore us. Just as queer nights blossomed at straight bars as gay bars died off, services for queer folks began to appear in mainstream orgs as our own spaces floundered.

I hope Kendall found them.

A little while after he was banned, maybe a year and a half after I was hired, Deb pulled me into her office, panicked. She was a soft butch Latina from the Bronx, and I'd never seen her flustered. "I'm out," she told me. She'd been working at the center for more than a decade and had overseen our integration with New York City's government; when it was complete, the straight supervisor the city installed looked at her résumé and said she didn't have the experience for her position. They picked her apart with demerits until she knew it was leave or get fired. "You have to stop them," she said. A group of us tried to form a union, but it went nowhere. The only piece of paper in my HR file from the years I worked at the center was a letter threatening to fire us for organizing. We started hemorrhaging staff: Some were picked off by admin, some left when they realized they were hired with false promises, and many just burned out.

The kids picked up on our bad energy. Even with fewer youth every day, the fights got worse. "Unstructured socialization" didn't win government grants, but in truth, what youth needed from us was a safe place with adults who cared about them, not a room full of new rules and new ways not to be good enough. One afternoon, two big bruisers got into a real one, and they didn't slow down when I stepped between them. By the time we wrestled them apart, my arms were covered in cuts, bruises, and blood. Both students were HIV positive, but when I tried to tell my supervisor I needed to go to the hospital to get postexposure HIV-prevention meds, she told me I didn't have the proper HIPAA authorization to discuss the serostatus of those students—and besides, there was no one to take over my shift.

I cleaned off the blood as best I could in the bathroom and got back to work. That night, I told my roommates I was going to die in this job, but in the morning, I went back to the office.

A few months later I quit. I'd careened from academia to direct service work with neither a plan nor much in the way of training, and I realized I needed to pause before I threw myself wholeheartedly into another mistake.

I kept in touch though. I heard about it when Ksen got into law school, and when Joseph killed himself, and when Carlos—who had been Angel, and then Carlos, and then Angel again—got promoted to manager of that Au Bon Pain on 8th Street. Tenaja and I became actual friends eventually, and the great divide between us as student and staff turned out to be just five years. The center teetered for a while, stretched thin between what youth needed it to be and what some administrators and funders wanted it to be. But surprisingly, it righted itself. Dinner was restored, as were the drop-in center, pantry, and supportive services. No one was saved, but blessedly, the work continues.

I left, but the center never left me. I found ways to return, year in and year out. When I started a pop-up museum, we did a fashion show with the ballroom kids and an exhibit of photos about AIDS made by some of the students. As a journalist, I interviewed students and staff for stories about gender, television, voguing, the history of AIDS, and more. They had become part of my world and part of the way I see the world too. They showed me there were other ways to divide the pie of sexuality and gender, and that allowed me to see how different ideas about queerness were throughout history and across the globe. Even in the moments when I was jealous of the freedoms they had, I knew I was blessed to be part of their community. And that blessing was also a commitment: They had opened my eyes, and in return, it would be my job to keep them open.

I felt certain I'd run into Kendall again, on the street outside the center one day when I dropped by to visit Juli, or on the subway six years later, the way I ran into Amarilys on the R train one morning, and even though she was twenty-six now and hadn't seen me in half a decade, she gave me a full rundown on her housing, her health insurance, and her job hunt. But no. I never saw Kendall again. And because I never knew his real name, I couldn't look him up later, once social media took off. He was just gone, like the gayborhoods I grew up through and the twentieth century itself.

Kendall, I don't know if you'll ever see this, or if you'd even remember me if you did. But I want you to know I remember you and that I don't go a day without thinking about that intense queer world we cocreated, our trial run for a new future, messy and beautiful, on the third floor of an anonymous building in lower Manhattan, a place the straight world walked by a million times and never once noticed.

All the Wrong Words

THIS WAS A TIME WHEN LANGUAGE OFTEN FAILED ME—when I never knew the right words, or the right words didn't exist. And yet also when I began to see language as my salvation.

Mr. Big Cock Europe 2003 was drunk. At 9 a.m. Again.

It was 2004, my first week in Berlin, and Tang (Mr. Big Cock) had taken me to one of the small bridges that crossed the Spree, the river dividing West from East, to teach me to ride a bike. I'd always been scared of things that moved too fast—bikes, horses, cars, life—because I was certain I'd fall and crack my skull open. I liked to keep one foot on the ground. But after quitting my job with queer youth and breaking my lease in Brooklyn (screwing over my roommates in the process), I'd decided to embrace free fall and see what happened. Maybe my skull needed cracking: a trepanning to release the twentieth century.

My friend Caeriel had fallen in love with a New Zealish drag queen named Princess Hans and followed him to Berlin. I was not in love and had no particular interest in Germany, which I associated with things I disliked (rules, Nazis, beer), but I was excited to surf the wake of Caeriel's drive. Caeriel was a writer who had for years eked out a living off a syndicated newspaper astrology column. As we became friends, I watched over his shoulder as the internet killed that business model; moving to Berlin was a way of putting it on hospice care, stretching his shrinking checks a little further. I wanted to be him, or I wanted to be him ten years ago when he was just starting out, or I wanted to leech from him the ability to figure out what I wanted and go get it.

But I settled for being his sidekick for a while.

Caeriel arrived in Berlin first and found us a temporary sublet, and he invited Tang, an old friend whose path he hadn't crossed in years, to a welcome party on my first night in town. Tall, blond, and beautiful, Tang looked like Captain America just gone to seed. A soft layer of chub covered him, giving him a cherubic affect and a great ass. He had a big goofy smile and called everyone "cuzzin," but he was filled with a sour sadness—a sense that life had passed him by or was flying past him right that very instant. He'd had a great gig as an escort-about-Europe for the last few years, but now that Poland was joining the European Union, "those boys would do anything for €50," he complained when drunk. Which he was, always, when I knew him. I didn't know that yet, though, so when he suggested that I learn to ride a bike on the narrow neutral zone between two lanes of whizzing traffic on a small bridge, I didn't protest.

The night before, we'd had a boring threesome with a German actor named Martin; I hadn't realized it was a trick until Martin gave Tang a wad of cash—and me, his old bike, which he hadn't used since landing a TV show and buying a car. Upon learning I couldn't ride, Tang declared he'd teach me. There was something tender and controlling about it: dad-like, in a way that usually turned me off, but on Tang it was hot, or maybe that's just what I was looking for that spring. I wanted his big hands to catch me, hold me, mold me, edge me.

He was, unfortunately, a real person, not a projection to satisfy my needs—and also, a terrible teacher. After positioning me on the bike, he slapped my ass to send me jolting toward traffic and yelled, "If you fall, you'll die!"

I could have sworn those were my words in his mouth, that he'd licked them off my lips the night before.

My look that year was baby-faced fetishist, anarchist himbo, ragamuffin slut. I lived in a pair of tight green ultra-low-rise leather Diesel pants that flared at the ankle and gathered to a drawstring crotch, which I paired with a sleeveless fishnet shirt, or a long black women's vinyl jacket à la Trinity from *The Matrix*, or nothing but body glitter and a velveteen dog collar. Whenever we were bored, I let Caeriel take scissors to my hair—now bleach blond mohawk; now purple spikes; now entirely shaved but for a rat tail and long, curly payot.

My spiritual inspiration was a young guy who lived in our neighborhood in East Berlin. He had curly black hair and dusky skin, and he wore raccoon makeup and dirty white ballet flats with comically overlong ribbon ties that he wound up his legs and around his body, like a sexy, disheveled mummy. He had the unhinged air of a peripatetic saint. Crowds parted around him, and when they reformed in his wake, all eyes darted back to him: angry, confused, aroused. His look provoked attention but forestalled interactions.

I wanted some of that holy fire. To be in the world and untouched by it at the same time.

Instead, I ended up on a German dating show, where they interviewed people on the street and invited viewers at home to email the station if they wanted to meet up. I received zero emails, but my episode was on opposite the 2004 EuroCup soccer game where Germany unexpectedly got destroyed by the Czech Republic, so for a while I convinced myself no one saw it. Then, in line for some mega club one night, I watched two guys discussing me at a distance. "You're talking about me," I said, pulling on one of their sleeves.

"Jas!" he said. "You were on the TV!" His English was barely better than my German, and the line was moving fast; he kept saying, "Hund, hund," trying to get me to understand. As we separated, he yelled, "All around gay Berlin, you are known as a collared dog!"

So I guess *that's* why no one emailed.

Our plan was we'd sell T-shirts on the streets of Europe, make money punky hand over artsy fist. Caeriel's friend Jim screen-printed beautiful shirts in the style of vintage vacation souvenirs, except his destinations were all places the US military was currently bombing. "Ski Iraq," one read, and another, "Greetings from Fallujah." It was an obtuse political statement that certainly went over the heads of the hipsters back on Orchard Street who paid upward of $100 a shirt. These were vintage-esque ringer tees from American Apparel, and they delighted the ironic trucker hat crowd who'd never be caught dead wearing a souvenir shirt from a place they'd *actually* visited. Plus, after 100,000 people marched through Manhattan in March 2003 to protest the ongoing military debacle in Iraq, anything that opposed "Dubya" and his murderously stupid administration was an easy sell in NYC (even if the message was confusing). By the time Caeriel and I were headed to Berlin in the spring of 2004, Bush's approval rating was the lowest it would be until Hurricane Katrina sent it underwater. The more the United States hated Bush, the better Jim's shirts did, so he agreed to sell us a bulk of them at cost, which we could resell at whatever price we wanted—a kindness to an old friend *and* a test run for a European operation.

Our plan was a flop. Turns out, Berlin was broke, and nobody wanted to spend $100 on a shirt. Or even $35. Also, the shirts were in English, and while everyone in Berlin spoke English, buying a shirt in English would have been seen as a weird, try-hard affectation. We spent two long days with our shirts spread on a blanket at a *flohmarkt* in a parking lot, selling nothing, and after that Caeriel got pissy. He was never one to linger on a hard decision. He had French citizenship in the works and would soon be able to get a legit job anyway, and while only a few papers still published his column, that was a little *something-something* every month. We made a few more half-assed attempts, but by my second week in Berlin, our T-shirt business was pretty much DOA. (Of course, I never considered selling them on my own; that wasn't the point of this exercise.)

Our plan? Caeriel's plan really. Here's the truth: I never expected the T-shirt thing to work. Insomuch as *I* had a plan, it was to float for as long as possible; see where I was when I ran out of gas. If you have no goals, it's impossible to fall short. All spring and summer, I wore my aimlessness like armor. For most of my teens and twenties, I had a pattern (though I couldn't see it) of structuring my life around one intense friendship at a time, almost always with another queer guy, for a year or two and then moving on—as I would soon with Caeriel. These relationships weren't sexual, but something erotic often hung in the air around them, making them intense, off-kilter, and unsustainable . . . but also powerful, capable of launching us halfway across the world together. They existed somewhere outside the paradigms of male relationships—neither wingmen, fuckbuddies, nor bros, but partaking of all those things. The closest analogue would be the great predatory homosexuals of the mid-twentieth century: Leopold and Loeb, Pauline Parker and Juliet Hulme, Tom Ripley and Dickie Greenleaf.

Minus the murder, of course.

In many ways, Berlin was a lot like New York—edgy, dirty, and full of queer weirdos—but it was much, much cheaper. Any night of the week, I could get dinner for €2 at a *VoKü* (short for *Volksküche*, or people's kitchen). A network of glorious squats riddled both halves of the city, like vibrant fungus giving new life to a lightning-split tree, and the *VoKü* were their most visible expression. There were no menus; €2 got you a plate of whatever they were serving that night. At some, another two would get you a never-ending glass of rotgut wine. X-B, the queer women's squat, had the best vegetarian food because only lesbians and people of Asian descent know how to cook tofu.

The squats and the numerous city parks had the same strange origin: the detritus of World War II. Despite the Marshall Plan, there simply wasn't enough money to put the city back together, and so in the following decades, many bombed buildings were razed for green space, while others were given to the people living in them, on the condition they make them *legally* livable. But the squat scene really exploded in the economically depressed Seventies, when hundreds of them appeared in the city. New York's squat scene had also boomed then, but they were mostly gone by the time I moved to NYC. In Germany, though, when the economy stagnated in the early 2000s (part of the global aftermath of 9/11), the squats rose to prominence again, and it was largely through them that I survived for five months on just the few thousand dollars I'd saved before I left New York.

In America, the movement for gay marriage was sucking all the political oxygen from queer organizing, but in Berlin the activists I met were focused on collective liberation, the creation of queer spaces, and, occasionally, defending everything they had gained over the past few decades from hordes of neo-Nazis, who would pour in from the suburbs to attack the squats. I had expected to find different answers to the questions that came with our emerging queer public world, but in Berlin they seemed to be asking different questions entirely. It was a scene full of big dirty dogs on rope leashes, cheap xeroxed zines, "free boxes," anarchist patches, mutual aid concerts, strung-out sweeties, activists with good politics and cruel hearts, and the omnipresent musk of cigarettes, BO, and stale beer. All of Berlin seemed broke in a good-natured way, and as a result ne'er-do-wells from around the world descended on the city in packs to practice their most useless skill and kill time until a better plan came along. Bustling without hustling, that was Berlin. Or at least, that was the side of it I saw.

Along with food, the squats had great parties. Black Girls Coalition (BGC)—run by two Black queens from the United States, Paisley Dalton and Krylon Superstar—was my favorite; it was there I heard "Comfortably Numb" covered by the Scissor Sisters for the first time. BGC was inspired by and took their name from a collective of mutual support among Black supermodels in the 1990s. Dalton and Superstar wanted to bring that same supportive energy to the global queer weirdos in Berlin—with their own twist, of course. They banned speaking German in the club, a restriction that Berliners embraced like a humiliation fetish, and it was a favorite hot spot for queer travelers.

White Trash Fast Food was the best music venue, the center of the electroclash scene, where everyone wanted to look and sound like Peaches. And then there was a bar on the river we called the James Bond Bar, because if you stumbled out back at the end of the night, there was a weird platform over the water, underneath which was a dock where there was always one small speedboat, as though awaiting a getaway.

But it was Tuntenhaus—the fag squat—where I spent the most time, because I was dating this spindly Icelandic anarchist named M, who looked like a hot version of Gollum. M had been volunteering with Starhawk, the infamous queer witch of the '90s, as a human shield in Palestine. The colonization of Palestine wasn't something I knew about at all back then, but M could evangelize passionately on the miserable conditions he'd seen in the occupied West Bank. As a good anarcho-communist, he didn't believe a word of Starhawk's neopagan mumbo jumbo . . . *but*, he said, if she said go left, the machine-gun turrets were always to the right, and they all learned to follow her lead if they wanted to live.

Eventually M was arrested by the IDF, who took his passport and deported him back to Reykjavik. There, he worked for an old man who ran a thrift store; when the man died, M packed up the contents of the store in a WWII-era truck so he could drive back to Palestine, selling stuff as he went and avoiding all the obvious border crossings because he still didn't have a passport. He made it as far as Berlin before the truck died—conveniently in front of Tuntenhaus, where he moved in while he saved the money to fix the truck. Every night he'd pack some of his random stuff in a suitcase and set up sale at the back of a *VoKü*, which is how we met.

Later, someone told me his name was actually Icelandic slang for prostitute and that the suitcase thing was all a front, but I saw the news articles; the human shield stuff was real, and I loved his willingness to throw his breakable, matchstick body on the line. He loved it when I wrapped my belt around his neck and choked him out while we fucked, but he never knew how to say what he wanted, and so our sex had an edging, edgy quality to it. We never used condoms or even discussed them. Neither of us knew where the line was, and sometimes I worried I was going to kill him accidentally, but he'd cum so hard his entire body would spasm for minutes at a time, and how was I to say no to that?

"It's not about size," Tang said dismissively one night. "It's about attitude."

I was not a size queen by any means, but it seemed to me that if it mattered in any arena, it was the electoral process for Mr. Big Cock Europe.

In New York, Caeriel and I were adventure buddies. We did postmidnight multiborough scavenger hunts; 500-person illegal outdoor food fights; tasting tours to places with no menus in English. For a brief moment post-9/11, rents dropped, city demographics shifted, and New York had the kind of raggedy, communal fun that's only possible when life is affordable.

Caeriel made me alive to *that* city; how much you got out when you put a lot in; what you could do with a lot of time and not much money.

But what really bound us together was *Survivor.*

When we met, I was still coming down from my late-'90s "kill your television" era. TV was mostly sitcoms and soap operas back then, stilted, stake-less, and unreal. Plus, if you *did* love a show, you had to build your life around it—miss an episode, and good luck ever finding it again. TiVo, the home digital-recording system, was just coming on the scene. Caeriel was the first person I knew who had one. And gay people rarely made so much as a cameo in most shows. GLAAD didn't start its annual count of queer characters until 2005, the year after I was in Berlin, but that year they made up an abysmal 1.4 percent of the TV landscape (compare that to 2023, which saw a major decline in gay characters from the year before . . . and still we made up 8.6 percent of roles). Those queer characters who did see airtime in the '90s tended to be sexless and living circumscribed, plastic lives in which they had no gay friends and existed mostly as foils for the straight characters.

Reality TV was just starting to gain prominence, and in high school I had fallen hard for *The Real World* (the show about "seven strangers, picked to live in a house") because the third season had famously featured Pedro Zamora, who was very hot (and gay, and HIV positive, and a political badass). Zamora, to me, showed the promise of reality TV—no one was writing gay Cuban Americans with AIDS as complex protagonists in network shows in those days, that was for sure. But reality *competition* shows, like *Survivor*, seemed—well, trashy. I was publicly disinterested, but I'd heard a gay villain had won the first season, and that intrigued me. Caeriel still had to trick me into watching the 2003 premiere by inviting me over for dinner. But by the end of the night, I was jumping on his couch howling at the TV, and we had a standing *Survivor* date for the rest of the season (Pearl Islands, the best non-all-star cast ever). My apartment was in Brooklyn, he lived in Queens, and we were so far-flung that the easiest route between us went through Manhattan and took ninety minutes each way on a good day. What I'm saying is: I got a lot of reading done every Thursday from then on, and isn't that the mark of a great friendship? Plus, with the commute always looming, it was easy to push the end of the night later and later, until often I just slept on his floor. In this way we nurtured the kind of unplanned time that deepens the relationships of children, siblings, and college students. Our friendship was a mix of doing Big Things and doing nothing, and we found ourselves in harmony at each step on that scale.

But moving to Berlin together, living together, and trying to work together all at once was too much. Whereas previously we often *chose* to spend twelve or twenty-four hours together, now we were forced to, and that constant closeness made it hard to plan adventures. We saw each other all the time, after all, so it felt natural to make plans instead with other people. Plus our relationship now had to encompass the kinds of decisions that couples face: picking out apartments (we moved four or five times over the course of our stay); launching and shutting a business. All these unexpected changes stressed our relationship, and we tried to ignore it because talking about a friendship—what it means or how much it means to you—is considered weird, the kind of thing only obsessive horse girls do. *Friend* is such a squishy, useless term; we use it for people we haven't seen in twenty years and people we'd give our kidneys to. Because there was no good word for our relationship, it was impossible to discuss or acknowledge, and therefore to fix. It was a dog with no name, and when it turned, all we could do was put it down.

What did I want out of our relationship? I wasn't really certain, or it seemed like what I wanted wasn't right to want. Best friends forever. A lonely child's wish. Over and over again, I'd crank the dial to eleven on a friendship and fry it out, while simultaneously using it as an excuse to drop the life I'd been living and strangle a dozen other friendships in the cradle. In a world where even gay people were increasingly becoming focused on coupledom and marriage, the weight I put on friendship seemed stranger and stranger (even to me). But what I had not yet come to understand was this: There was a time when I had few friends, and because of that I longed for unbreakable bonds; but in those same years, I became a full person, a loner originally more by circumstance than choice, but now a loner nonetheless. As an adult, making friends came easily to me, but I didn't—and wouldn't, for a long time—understand what it took to *keep* a friend. Worse: I didn't understand that I didn't like having a lot of friends; that I found friendship exhausting and had a lot of things that I wanted to do by myself. It would take a decade, and several more turns on this particular ride, before I'd learn that lesson.

How much of that is just my personal predilection and how much is the result of being entombed in the thick skin you needed to survive as a gay person back then, I'll never know.

But there is a certain rootlessness among many of my queer friends my age. My straight(er) friends were getting married, or at least sliding down the road to it, and we were still spinning, out there somewhere, unsure how or where or if to land. New possibilities for queer existence were opening all around us—places becoming safer, blood families becoming more accepting, the whole new world of marriage existing at all—but we'd been running the old track for so long, we approached these new ones with a gimlet eye. None of it felt real, or reliable, or open to us. We may have changed the world, but changing ourselves was trickier.

As American gays mainstreamed, the places I loved—the secretive gay bars, the queer youth centers, the Radical Faerie sanctuaries—were dismissed with a sneer as backward, separatist, and a little embarrassing. Right before I left the country, *New York* magazine profiled our center with a cover story that declared we shouldn't exist. But in Berlin, queer collectives were hot spots. There was a gay museum and a lesbian archive in development; there were so many queer sex parties that the listings in the free gay magazines had to be divided into categories so you didn't accidentally bring your electro-stim toys to the mummification party. I first began to see a desirable future in the squats of Berlin: neither rootless and alone nor a poorly aped version of heterosexuality. But it would take many more years to bring that vision to fruition.

One evening, Caeriel, Hans, and I were out walking, waiting for the night city to wake up, when we came across a British woman in a Donna Karan power suit, crying on the steps of a bank. She was looking for an ATM; she had, just an hour before, told her husband she wanted a divorce, and now she needed a new hotel. It was their sixth and final night in Berlin, and once again, he'd refused to go out; after two-ish decades of this, with her fifties on the near horizon, she couldn't take it anymore.

"Anna," she said by way of introduction. Then she grabbed her breasts from underneath and made them jiggle at the neckline of her jacket. "Like Nicole Smith!"

And with that, she burst into tears again.

ATMs were rare in Berlin then, or perhaps, having no money, we just didn't know where they were. Either way, after a brief consultation, we asked Anna to tag along with us. Where? Wherever.

She was Alice, and we, the rabbit hole. She dived in. Deep.

We went to one place, and then another, and another after that, until it was nearly sunup. As she sobered, Anna became progressively wilder, until *she* seemed to be the center that Caeriel, Hans, and I were pivoting around. She had cougar energy, hot and in charge. She had a way of meeting your eyes from across the room and silently communicating that it was on purpose—that she was in that very moment thinking of *you*—and at each venue we went to, a loose circle of new acquaintances found us.

Her husband must be a real pill, I thought to myself. And, *This is what we're fighting to get access to?*

We'd stumbled accidentally across an ATM at some point, and she had the money she needed to get a hotel, but when we decided our last stop of the night would be Rose's, a kitschy cluttered gay bar in Kreuzberg, she said she had to go, that it was fate. She owned a secondhand store called Rose's and had a tattoo of one on her hip. She pulled her jacket up and pants down to show me, then grabbed my hand and ran my fingers along it, and when she released me, my hand continued, tracing a shivery line down her hip bone. Then we kissed hard and went inside.

The walls of Rose's were covered in silk flowers and paintings of sad-eyed kids with benevolent angels rising above them. Her lips were very soft but her tongue insistent. Probing. In between, she had so many questions: A friend of hers had recently died of AIDS. Was he going to hell? Was she going to hell for being his friend? Her husband said so. But once in college she'd had sex with a girl, her best friend, and it had been incredible, and it was that—wasn't it?—that she was going to hell for.

Men or women, cis or trans, queer or straight: I've always been a magnet for the sexually ambivalent; the ones without labels for what they are, or want, or want to be. "Hell's just a word," I told her. "Maybe this is hell."

At one point she whispered in my ear, "I have a son your age," and that seemed to turn us both on. Then she unlaced my leather pants, and we fingered each other like exuberant teenagers, until we both came under the eyes and glowing sword of the archangel Michael.

"What's a guardian angel anyway?" she asked Caeriel, and Hans, and the bartender, and everyone else still left as the bar shut down, but we didn't have any answers. We got her a taxi, and the last I ever saw Anna, she was shoving the top half of her body out the car window, screaming, "You're my guardian angels! You're my guardian-fucking-angels!" as around her fluoresced the first dawn of her new life.

Later, I'd learn I'd misheard the guy in line: not *collared* dog but *colorful* dog. "Bunter Hund," that's what the guy had been saying. It was the German equivalent of saying I stuck out like a tall poppy, not that I looked like a fucking dog.

Still, no one emailed me.

Over the months I was in Berlin, Caeriel and I played approximately 450 games of Scrabble. They started off collegial and fun, but two-thirds of the way through the summer, when it became obvious we were very closely matched, we got weird about it. If, in April, one of us had put down D-G-O by accident, the other would have flipped the order of the tiles and continued the game; by June, a mistake like that would be challenged, and whoever played it would lose their turn—and as a result, probably the game as well. After that, the air in our sublet would get rancorous, and one of us would soon find a reason to leave. Our connection was so activity-forward, so . . . *boy,* we'd never learned to have deep conversations about anything—which suited me just fine (unfortunately) but made our whole endeavor precarious (as my tied tongue did with every relationship I had).

After a bad game, if it was night, I'd go find M or Tang, but if the sun was still up, I was more likely to wend my way over to Another Country, my favorite English-language bookstore. At Another Country, all the books had two prices: one to buy and one to borrow. Usually it cost only €1 to borrow a book, and I often picked books by page count, to make them last.

The first time I walked in, I delighted the proprietor by asking if they had a copy of *Claudius the God*. I'd just finished *I, Claudius*, a gift from my parents, one of my father's favorite books in college. It was gayly homophobic in a very mid-century English way (much like its author, noted bisexual nympho Robert Graves). A euro lighter, I walked out the door with a dinged-up paperback copy so old I could imagine my father reading it at Manhattan College. When I returned a few days later, I swapped it for Barbara Kingsolver's *Poisonwood Bible*, which the proprietor recommended and my mother had loved. From then on, every time I visited, we'd chat about books; idle persiflage, nothing serious. But I looked forward to those trips, and they provided a periodicity to my stay in Berlin. Tick, tock, tick, tock; book, walk, book, walk: my life like a metronome, measuring nothing but itself. It was languorous, something that New York City—with its 24/7 subway, its manic millionaire dreams, and its biomythology as the city that never sleeps—wasn't capable of being. In Berlin, the present moment seemed always to take precedent, because everyone's future felt dim, or uncertain, or located far away. I unwound a little with every visit, lingered longer, until soon a trip to Another Country could take all day. There was something glorious and childlike about having to choose just one book, and I savored that limitation.

But despite all our interactions, I could remember nothing—not a single thing—about the person who owned Another

Country. Not their face or voice or gender or name. When I looked up the store to write this, I discovered that a decade after I'd known her, the owner had come out as a trans woman, and I blessed my memory for erasing what I thought I knew to make way for what actually was.

I was trying to follow Caeriel's lead, but it was impossible. He moved through the city like a spy trying to lose the guy on his tail, taking hard turns and crossing streets willy-nilly. He moved through the city like there was no one behind him at all.

Emboldened by surviving Tang's death-defying lesson, I'd decided to take the bike out that night. But after five minutes following Caeriel, I drove straight into a street sign and cratered to the ground. My knee swelled up like a grapefruit, and I never touched the bike again that summer. I went home, and Caeriel continued on.

This is both metaphor and literal truth, and there are days when my whole Berlin life seems tinged with this golden aura of significance, every event divinely ordered or deeply coded with meaning I couldn't read at the time. But probably I was just young and in love with living, my back never hurt, and I was jaded only in the foppish, faddish way of young people.

Several times I asked M to teach me Icelandic, but it sounded like wet paper being torn or birds vomiting. It was a language so liquid I couldn't even sense the edges of the words as he spoke them slowly. Finally, I asked him to teach me just a single saying; something to remember him by; something I could use in real life.

He thought for a moment, then trilled out a short, incomprehensible song. "What does that mean?" I asked.

"The mountain woman sweeps away the evils of capitalism with her skirts."

I couldn't memorize it, because I couldn't pronounce a single syllable of it. But I've never found anyone who's ever heard of this saying, so for all I know, he made it up on the spot.

After a few months like this, some things became clear. As much as I loved certain classes at Cornell or working with my students at the center, I hated a high-stakes life. I didn't want to constantly be afraid of falling. I wanted to be alone more and matter less. I was the tail end of Gen X, but still, that slacker energy had infused me at a young age. "Whatever" was our halfhearted rallying cry, our *yawn de coeur*, and I was ready to embrace it.

One day, feeling aimless, I made a long list of things that I wanted out of life, some silly ("to be able to wear pajamas all day if I want"), some overwrought ("to make the world a better place"), but all of them true. Then I made another list: What was I good at? Then I spent a long time wondering how I could use the skills on List 2 to get the things on List 1. For a while, I considered becoming a graphic/web designer, like half the people I knew in New York. But I was only marginally talented at both those things, and while that hadn't stopped me from getting piecemeal work throughout college, I wasn't sure my ego could handle doing something where I wasn't praised on a regular basis. Honors student syndrome or just stupid pride, call it what you want, but it was true.

So there was only one option: write.

Writing had always hovered in the periphery of my mind, the way a child dreams of dessert before they even get to the dinner table. It was something I could have years from now, when I'd eaten all the spinach life could throw at me. My mother loved to write, and she was great at it, and she always said one day—when she retired—she would write mystery novels (which, eventually, she did). But back then, writing felt more like a fantasy, not a job. It certainly wasn't something I could pursue or improve at.

Except there was Caeriel, in the next room over, doing exactly that. He wanted to write fantasy novels, but he wrote astrology columns because he knew astrology, and it was a niche that he realized could be lucrative.

What was my niche? Mostly useless school stuff. But over the last few months I'd perfected being a broke expat (which is what magazines call migrants when they're White), and so I sold myself as an expert on Berlin. Most real editors saw right through me, but this was still a time of relative abundance, especially in Europe, before the internet had completely scythed print culture, and I sent queries to dozens of places in order to land one or two gigs. My writing was mediocre, my pitches were worse, and I didn't understand how to take print-resolution digital photos, despite my assurances otherwise to editors. I wrote about the *VoKü*, the *flohmarkts*, and the city's street festivals. I fumbled a lot, but I was fumbling forward.

I landed my first lasting gig toward the end of my time in Berlin, writing for a Canadian advertising company that pretended to be a wedding magazine. Their schtick was "reality wedding journalism," but not a word of it was true. I know, because sometimes I wrote nearly the entire issue. As far as I was aware, they had no editor or any other staff, just a director of marketing; occasionally I was paid to pretend to be the editor, writing her columns and even her correspondence, though I drew the line when they wanted me to appear in person at a conference as "an assistant authorized to speak on her behalf." I worked for them on and off for the next three years. I discovered I was a good ventriloquist; with a pen in hand I could sound like anyone—six different people in an issue, if I needed to. It's part of what makes me so good at skiting across the surface of the world, the way my chameleon tongue drifts toward whomever I'm around. But it's also why writing, for me, is so solitary; the more I listen to other people, the less I can hear myself. My best writing days are ones where I'm at my desk before I read the news or talk to anyone; they fall apart the moment I touch Twitter.

Writing for them unexpectedly taught me something else: Every glance I got under the hood of marriage, it seemed like a bum deal that wasn't going to get us anywhere good. Sure, I hated being discriminated against, who doesn't. But wasn't all marriage law a kind of discrimination, based on sexual relationships? I understood why the government wanted to give tax breaks to people who took care of each other—that made simple economic and policy sense. But the squats did that work as well (or better) than Anna's marriage, without an entire fucking industry of lies and beauty standards propping them up, so why were American gays racing to the altar?

It was a real head-scratcher to me, but for a while, I was happy to take their money.

In the middle of my stay in Berlin, my parents, brothers, a couple of aunts, and a few cousins all flew to Ireland, where they traveled along the River Shannon, visiting our farther-flung relatives for a few weeks. Caeriel and I met them in Galway for the annual arts festival. Shockingly, our shirts sold well there, as there was an active street busker scene (and people actually spoke English). Our most popular read, "Where Would Jesus Bomb?" and featured falling missiles with the face of George W. Bush on them. A turn in the political winds was happening, and you could sense it strongly when you went abroad—Bush was a laughingstock, and the delight of the Irish in mocking him seemed to augur good things.

On our second-to-last day, Caeriel saw a poster with a name he recognized: Heather Woodbury, an artist from New York City. She was presenting a multipart epic, a "living novel," where she wrote and performed every character in a one-woman maelstrom spanning 100 years and the entirety of the United States. We could only catch the first part—and that alone was four hours.

For 240 minutes, Woodbury possessed my soul; though she was the only person on stage, every word she spoke came to life in my mind. I felt a click inside me: *This*—I wanted to do *this*. I had needed to come to writing as a practical decision (I always like to keep one foot on the ground), but this was the spark that kept me going through the long years when nothing I wrote was good and nothing sold. Sure, maybe I didn't know *how* to write, but I knew how to tell a story—the amusing anecdote was my global currency in those years—and I knew with enough work I could harness that ability. A dim outline of a life appeared to me in the Irish gloaming: journalism to get a start, stories (or what I would later learn to call personal essays) as a career. It didn't work out that simply of course; I ended up going to grad school for an MFA and then getting sidetracked into ghostwriting shitty kids' books for five years. But it was a necessary vision, a road map that I could refer to whenever I felt lost, even if I wasn't following it to the letter.

I clipped Woodbury's bio from her program, and months later, when I was back in New York, I began tracing her footsteps.

It's been a long trip to this very moment; a circuitous, twenty-year route to untie my tongue. For a time this made me feel pathetic, or perhaps . . . guilty? A failure, or an underachiever, at least. But now I think it's the only way I could have gotten here.

Caeriel and I had a falling out—in IKEA, of course, the place you go to trade your relationship for a down-market couch.

The trip was doomed from the beginning. Berlin's subway worked on the Stasi system. There were no gates to stop you from getting on without a ticket. But the government employed average citizens as plainclothes *Kontrollers*, who would wait until the train was between stations, stand up, announce the car was being "kontrolled," and pull out their ticket-checking machines. They issued fines on the spot (€100 or more) and kicked you off the train.

I played the subway like a slot machine; I probably bought five tickets over the five months I was in Berlin. That morning, I convinced Caeriel he didn't need a ticket, or maybe I told him I had one when I didn't? Either way, I fucked us up, and when the *Kontroller* announced himself, we split up to avoid him, and I ended up running onto the platform. I saw Caeriel through the window as the subway pulled away, making a complicated series of hand gestures at me. Then he was gone, and I was left in a far part of Berlin that I didn't know at all. Worse, my wallet was in his bag (my leather pants didn't have pockets). For a while, I waited for him to come back, but he didn't, so I got on another train, figuring eventually I'd be able to see the IKEA and know where to get off. But as the train pulled out of the next station, I realized Caeriel was sitting there, waiting for me. With some more frantic gesturing, we devised a plan and successfully met up at the next station. But we were snarly now, like hangry cats, and our adventure had turned into a trudge.

Caeriel needed a lamp because he was staying in Berlin, and even if he continued subletting furnished apartments, he wanted a little pocket of comfort he could bring with him, a guarantee that he could read in bed. What I was doing at IKEA was unclear, other than hanging on Caeriel's coattails, but he wanted me to weigh in on his choices. My money was dwindling, and it was impossible to get a real job in Berlin—or a cell phone, or a bank account, or even to receive mail—without having some kind of visa; following Caeriel's lead again, I'd started the process of applying for Irish citizenship, but that, it turned out, would take years.

For an hour, slogging through the showroom, we disagreed about everything. Finally, after we had rejected every lamp in IKEA and a few they had yet to invent, I threw up my hands. "Do what you want," I said bitterly. "I'm not staying anyway."

That was obviously true by this point. I'd never found my footing, and my half year in Berlin hadn't turned into anything more than an extended, soul-searching vacation. But Caeriel and I had never discussed it.

Our current sublet would be up soon. I'd drifted away from Tang by that point, and M had started quietly dating a mutual friend. Our T-shirts hadn't seen the sun in months. I had this sudden sense, standing in the windowless, climate-controlled IKEA marketplace, of a rush of air—the feeling of free fall.

Caeriel bought a lamp, and a few weeks later I was back in New York.

I did eventually learn to ride a bike, a few years later, during a brief stop back in Brooklyn between Asheville and Puerto Rico, thanks to my friend Megan. She was a tiny redhead with anger-management issues and a great sense of humor; she played trombone in the Rude Mechanical Orchestra (a "radical marching band"), and I was part of their dance team, Tactical Spectacle. We played fundraisers for mutual aid societies, protested un-unionized work sites, and occasionally acted as a distraction or hype machine at large-scale protests of the G8 or the Republican National Convention. We had been tear-gassed together in Pittsburgh and would eventually hack a school bus to make it run on biodiesel so we could travel across the country protesting Republicans in 2008. Who needed gay marriage when you had a bus full of sparkly anarchists on your side? We weren't a specifically queer band, but when straight people joined, they tended to give up their heterosexuality, at least for a little while, like Catholics skipping meat for Lent.

Once, I'd run into Megan on a bad day—her girlfriend had broken up with her, and she'd lost her cell phone in the Gowanus Canal. So I gave her mine for a week. Ever since, we'd looked out for each other, even if sometimes our band's eight-hour, consensus-based meetings drove us to screaming at each other.

"This is the one essential thing you gotta know to ride a bike," Megan said solemnly, as we stood on the grass holding our bicycles. "Repeat after me: Go fuck yourself. A car cuts you off in traffic? Go fuck yourself. Some guy tries to tell you you need a fixed-gear-hoo-ha-whatnot to be a *real* cyclist? GO. FUCK. YOUR. SELF!"

She had me practice yelling "Go fuck yourself" until the nannies in Prospect Park were taking wide circles around us, and I had all the room in the world to pedal unsteadily on the grass, or the path, or to drift back and forth between the two, and suddenly I looked up and *she* was following *me*, and then I fell and it was hilarious and I shouted, "Go fuck yourself," at myself.

And then I got back up and pedaled away.

My Bad

FOR MOST OF MY TWENTIES AND EARLY THIRTIES, I LIVED like a yo-yo. After returning from Berlin with Caeriel, I left Brooklyn for Puerto Rico (with Lenni); then I went to house-sit a place in the winter in upstate New York on my own; then I moved back to the city to be with Angelo; then I moved to Asheville, North Carolina (where Caeriel had landed after he and Princess Hans broke up); then Brooklyn again . . .

My pattern had become obvious: I'd spin out to spend six months here or there, but I always snapped back to New York, the only place I'd ever put down roots, because they were there before my guard went up. Then something would go wrong—usually a breakup of some kind, friend or lover—and I'd fly off again.

Like that, eight years passed.

On its own, this circularity would have been troubling enough, but worse, my cycles seemed to be getting shorter and the patches of stability in between more ephemeral. Most recently, I had fucked over my best friend, Brian, by sleeping with his boyfriend because I was—shocker—in love with Brian, and somehow in the aftermath of all that, he and I decided to move to Puerto Rico together, where he accused me of being in love with said boyfriend, and I exploded into laughter and told Brian that no, I was in love with *him*. After a long, awkward silence, we decided to go our own ways. I ended up in New Orleans, doing my best impression of an alcoholic; Brian moved to Brazil and lived on a monkey sanctuary.

When, inevitably, I washed back up on the coast of Brooklyn, I was thirty-two, and the new century was a leggy ten-year-old, already racing forward. We were two years into the Obama administration, and although the world had not transformed overnight, there was a sense that perhaps we had managed to fix things just a little, or that we had at least begun a path that could, in the nebulous but not *too* distant future, lead to a great unfucking of the world. This was naive—that path, it turned out, would lead us straight into the maw of the orange-skinned ogre from Queens. But that Shepard Fairey poster had made "hope" the watchword of the moment, and even I was optimistic. The halfhearted toleration of the '90s—Don't Ask, Don't Tell; domestic partnerships—was out of vogue, and real change seemed to be happening. Obamacare could have gone further, but it was at least a bold attempt to restructure a broken institution. Marriage equality wouldn't have been the battle I chose, but love (and the wedding industrial complex) was winning, so what did I know?

But same-sex marriage wouldn't much change life for most of us, though friends got pissy and called me a killjoy (correctly) when I pointed that out. I had just a few hundred dollars in my bank account, a suitcase worth of clothing, and a sublet room in a large, illegally converted loft below a sweatshop in deepest Brooklyn. What was marriage gonna do for me? I rose and slept to the chatter of sewing machines above me and mechanics below me, the perpetual industrial hum constantly reminding me of the great and cruel work that kept our megalopolis running.

Me? I ran on hard-boiled eggs from the Polish deli on the corner—two for a dollar—and kidney-damaging amounts of coffee. Monthly, I cobbled together enough work to pay rent, but I was dancing frantically just to stay still: today writing short-form service journalism about the best puddle-jumper planes in Australia (a place I'd never been), tomorrow channeling a doctor from Maine to write his paper for *The New England Journal of Medicine*. Occasionally I'd sell a short essay to one of the last alternative papers, like the *New York Press* (RIP), but I hadn't found my voice, so everything I wrote was a shallow David Sedaris manqué. When all else failed, I took a gig as a go-go boy or went dumpster diving at the bougie markets in Park Slope that took sell-by dates so seriously, they frequently dumped all their meat and dairy a day or two or three before it was even technically "bad" (and I only got food poisoning once—never eat a rotisserie trash chicken).

This was by choice; I had by this point many friends and family members who would have loaned me money, but I hated asking for it or being in debt to anyone, even if the other person didn't care. I lacked the strength to be vulnerable in that way; too much scar tissue on my heart. I didn't want to depend on something that could be taken back the moment someone disagreed with me. I'd sleep on their couches and store books in their basements, but I drew the line at cash. I sprinted through a series of agents—always attracted by my potential but underwhelmed by my reality—and wrote the first chapters of several books: a YA novel that was a queer take on Jumanji; a "reformed vegetarian's handbook" on how to source and cook ethical meat; a cultural history of monsters in America. In each case, I made it 30 percent through and found myself adrift, unsure of what I was doing or how to move forward. Over and again, I hit the same wall: They said, "Write what you know," but I didn't seem to know anything, or I knew lots of little things that didn't add up to any big thing in particular. Glitter and wit could get me only so far (about seventy pages, it seemed).

After a few months of this, I got antsy. My wandering feet were sore. I couldn't keep this up. I needed a change, a big one.

So I decided this time I'd leave the city by boat.

The financial crash of 2008 had devastated many communities, but perhaps none more so than hope-heads who bought boats they couldn't afford. "For Sale" signs on McMansions attracted more attention, but the abandoned boats of the formerly rich were turning up regularly on Craigslist and in the least-policed waterways near major cities. The crash took a wrecking ball to the financial hopes of Millennials; blame avocado toast all you want, but the explosion of the housing bubble—and the lack of change to the capitalist forces that allowed it to happen (and profited off it)—soured most young people I knew on the idea of the American dream. New possibilities would emerge from the wreckage, but it would take a while, so why not wander while that was happening?

I'd dipped my toe in boat life by dating a guy who lived in a dilapidated ferry on the toxic Gowanus Canal in Brooklyn, whose waters were so cursed he developed a yeast infection only seen among travelers in the Amazon. Through him I'd met some Cakalak anarchists, whom I spent time with while living in North Carolina; through them, I heard that some friends of friends were planning on squatting a boat and sailing to the Caribbean come winter. They were crewing up now while they scouted for just the right one—abandoned, undamaged, capable of sleeping six to ten people, with all its navigational thingamajammers still intact.

Years before, an older friend once said to me, "You wanna live on a boat? Go stand in the shower fully dressed while you tear up $100 bills. If you like that, go for it!"

But boat life appealed to me because if you traveled in your home, you could never be homeless; the closest I could get to a turtle existence.

"Are you kidding me?" my younger brother Jim replied when I told him.

He'd called to ask about my plans for Thanksgiving—meaning, how was I getting to our parent's house in the suburbs? We both lived in Brooklyn now, maybe twenty minutes apart as the crow flies, but on different subway lines and thus in different worlds. He'd come out, graduated from college, done a series of great internships, and gotten a good gig at Nerve, an edgy sex and dating website. They were part of a flourishing millennial online ecosystem, alongside Jezebel and Buzzfeed and everything else that once made the internet interesting. Jim had battled his way into that rarefied field right out of college. We were very similar people made from slightly different pieces: Jim had our mom's gray-blue eyes and a double helping of her anxiety; I, our father's hazel eyes and his knack for putting things out of mind (sometimes forever). But we had the same way with words and inability to hold our tongue when angry.

Surprised by Jim's vehemence, I got defensive. Who cared about Thanksgiving? It was a racist holiday dedicated to football and gluttony. Turkey was the driest of meats, the love child of chicken and sand. The only good thing about Thanksgiving was stuffing and Christina Ricci's Pilgrim-hunting monologue from *Addams Family Values*.

Jim huffed—half growl, half sigh, a mucosal sound of frustration I'd often heard crawl from my own throat—"When do you get back?"

"Uhhh . . . " there had been some talk of trying to spend New Years in the Caribbean, then making our way to Mexico . . .

"No," Jim cut me off. "No, you are too fucking old for this. Jesus, Hughie, mom and dad are too old for this."

As a point of fact, our parents were only in their mid-sixties—but my father had recently had prostate cancer, and though his recovery was complete, it had been slow. I'd been spared most of the particulars by being selfish and unreachable. But it was undeniably a turning point in their lives (and ours)—much as I was still trying to deny it.

Jim and I had fought before, over stupid things: where to go for brunch or our opinions about the TV show *Supernatural*. But for the first time, he was right.

Being wrong gnawed at me. Being stuck gnawed at me. But worse than anything, I now had enough experience to know that—stay or go—I'd never finish the projects I was "working" on, and without the thin facade of adventure, I was just . . . a quitter. Lazy, like Mrs. Keirnan had said in the fourth grade.

I was lazy, it was true, at least when it came to things that bored me. But also: Growing up in the '80s and '90s meant I hadn't much considered *having* a future, and so the work it took to have a dream and see it through to completion seemed—foreign? Inexplicable? Like a waste of fucking time, I'd learned that in college. And I wasn't the only one: I'd met so many queer artists who skated by on talent and personality, always telling me their big plans over coffee or on acid but never bringing anything to completion; so many forty-seven-year-old once-wunderkinds who, seeing few other options, had set fire to their futures and danced by that light, now peering at the embers and wondering what was left for them, of them. I could feel that hollowness growing in me, the inverse of cancer, a too-littleness instead of a too-muchness.

But even that metaphor was a dodge, an attempt to place blame on something uncontrollable—not myself, which I refused to control.

I texted Jim and told him I'd take the train up the day before Thanksgiving and spend the night at mom and dad's. He said he'd meet me at Grand Central Station.

Abandoning my imagined boat life left me feeling unmoored, and it was in this frustrated state that I heard about the Smithsonian Museum's censorship of David Wojnarowicz, one of my favorite artists of the twentieth century. Wojnarowicz's writings about AIDS, politics, and the suburbs were raw and angry; his paintings were layered and strange, combining houses on fire with plastic toys, skulls, hearts, cops, clocks, and cock rings—his personal symbolic language. He'd been a street hustler in Times Square starting at thirteen and died of AIDS and government neglect at thirty-seven. In between he'd channeled a luminous rage whose heat, it seemed, still made the establishment squirm.

Earlier in 2010, a video of Wojnarowicz's work was included in *Hide/Seek*, the first Smithsonian exhibit to ever look specifically at queer art. But around the time Jim and I were making plans for Thanksgiving, a hatchet job by a right-wing website attacked his work for being sacrilegious, and the Smithsonian caved overnight. Literally: The piece was removed twenty-four hours later, without discussing it with the curators of the exhibition. Like many large cultural institutions, the Smithsonian was staffed by incrementalist lefties, whose guilt over their own politics made them gullible to far-right trolls. Because they disagreed with conservatives in their hearts, they gave in quickly to them in public, in order to front some kind of useless, amoral, middle-of-the-road neutrality. It got them nowhere: Congressional Republicans still tried to defund the entire Smithsonian over the show. (We didn't know this was a trial run for how so many institutions would roll over in the face of Trump et al., but if there is one thing history has taught me, it's that queer people are always on the cutting edge of getting fucked over by fascists. We're trendy that way.)

This wasn't the first time Wojnarowicz had been censored, but things were different now—not enough to stop the Smithsonian from going belly up at the first sign of trouble but enough that they couldn't just sweep their cowardice under the rug. Wojnarowicz's censored film began popping up everywhere, to the point where two students made a website dedicated to all the places you could now see it. It felt like a fairy tale of resistance, with Wojnarowicz as the queer weed they could not uproot. Schools, galleries, and museums rallied around Wojnarowicz, just as years before other social service organizations had stepped up to help the queer young people that the center I worked at had turned away. Some friends began organizing counterprotests in DC, and I decided I'd join them, maybe see if I could write about the controversy.

The more I thought about it, though, the less interested I was in protesting the Smithsonian—not that they didn't deserve it; they lacked the courage of their convictions and sold out both the artists they exhibited and their own curators at the first possible moment. Wojnarowicz, who railed so eloquently against the elites of America, had once again been knifed in the back by them, and we were all poorer for it.

But . . . then what? After the counterprotests died down, where would I go to see Wojnarowicz's other work, or any historical queer art? Even in 2010, New York's major museums had abysmal records when it came to queer artists, closeting them in their wall texts, hiding their most explicit works, and almost never exploring "queer art" as a legible category overall.

Just a few years before, in 2007, one of the curators of the *Hide/Seek* exhibit had coauthored a survey of major New York City museums. They found that over the previous twelve years, most had mentioned LGBT themes in less than 5 percent of their shows; some had never mentioned them at all. And from my decade of traveling, I knew that benighted New York was *still* better than most other places. Queer artists were at least shown in group shows that downplayed (or ignored entirely) their sexuality or gender. Sometimes, once they were safely dead, they could even get a show of their own, like the 1997 Whitney retrospective of Keith Haring. In what passed for a rave for a queer artist in those days, *The New York Times* called the show "smart" and "exuberant" but described Haring's actual work as "deft, febrile, often expressive but thin-textured." It wasn't until the eighteenth paragraph of the review that his sexuality was mentioned, and overall, the author opined, "There may never be another Haring retrospective on this scale" as "his work isn't meant for museum scrutiny."

No place here for you, fag.

With all this swirling around, I found myself rereading *Close to the Knives*, the book that was my first encounter with David Wojnarowicz, when I came across a favorite passage that suddenly struck me in a new way.

> *The rich have interchangeable heads and their interpretations of law and religion are just as manufactured, false, interchangeable and disposable. . . . Because I am born into a created system of corruption does not mean I have to turn the other way when the fake moral screens are unfurled. I am just as capable of creating my own moral contexts.*

I had many times quoted the part about the heads of the rich, even Sharpied it onto a T-shirt once. But I had paid less attention to what came after: *I am just as capable of creating my own moral contexts.* This was a call for action. To turn my attention away from the Smithsonian's asshattery and moral turpitude. I thought about Roz, the butch who held my hand through every terrifying AIDS test in college; about that night in the bathroom of the Tunnel talking with that queen about gender; about the entire universe of ballroom that queer people of color had created; about queer rural communes and urban queer squats and faggots the world 'round. It seemed in retrospect that the best parts of my life had been a hopscotch through an archipelago of queer spaces—some as temporary as a held door and a knowing nod; others, oases I could return to again and again. Why did we need to be in their world, when ours was so much more exciting?

What if, instead of protesting *their* museum . . . we made our own?

I didn't know what that meant exactly. But wasn't that the point? To see what we could do or be when we turned away from the "created system of corruption" we were born into?

The idea probably would have lived and died in my head like so many others were it not for the spontaneous intervention of queer providence.

Around Thanksgiving, as I was deciding to stay in Brooklyn, an ad hoc group calling themselves QuORUM—Queers Organizing for Radical Unity and Mobilization—had decided to create a week of queer events, led by queer people, in queer private spaces all around New York. They were part of the same generation that planned the counterprotests around Wojnarowicz: queer young people who were organized, assertive, and outside the traditional structures of power, but not without resources or reach. Like me, they had come out just in time to kiss the tail end of the vast gay world that was crumbling in the face of assimilation and AIDS, and they were determined to create queer space even as the bars and bookshops continued to shut down. They had arranged art talks and movement workshops and BDSM panels, but they contacted my roommates because they had yet to find a space big enough to host an opening night party. They were expecting as many as 100 people over the course of the evening, and our large industrial loft had both the space to hold them and something of a storied history in queer Brooklyn. In the early 2000s, it had hosted a weekly queer experimental movie night and potluck vegan dinner on Wednesdays; our large living room was often loaned to queer groups that needed meeting space; and the loft had been home to occasional all-gender queer sex parties with names like The Big Bang (we were located on Starr Street).

Most of my roommates were, like me, "old" queers who at thirty-two or thirty-four had been around and around. Jon, Betsy, and I had done volunteer defense work at the same abortion clinic in Sunset Park. Betsy was a drummer in the anarchist marching band I danced with, and we had once spent a delightful weekend together rebuilding the floor at Bluestockings, the feminist bookstore in the Lower East Side. Ana was a documentarian who would go on to cofound an anarchist community center a few blocks from where we lived. Sage was training to be a queer-affirming herbalist and healer, and Tim was our resident straight ally, an actor / organic farmer who brought home hundreds of dollars of unsold microgreens every week from the farmers market in Union Square.

So when QuORUM asked to use our house for their opening night, the answer was an instantaneous and resounding no.

We were all old and tired of cleaning other people's lube off the bathroom floor. But as I started imagining this "pop-up museum of queer history," it seemed like the perfect opportunity, and my roommates said it was fine so long as I bottom-lined the event: planned it, cleaned up after it, handled the cops if they were called, etc.

QuORUM was excited by the idea, or at least they were excited to have our space and willing to go along with this thing that I couldn't fully explain but could monologue about passionately. This would be comeuppance for every nerd who never got to make a diorama of their favorite queer book in school and every artist with a passionate dyke side project that was constantly deemed too niche for exhibitions. It was about recognizing queer expertise and creating a space where we could enjoy it without worrying that we'd be kicked out for using the "wrong" bathroom or censored to cater to the fears of straight people.

The one problem was that I didn't know anything about art or art handling, so I didn't know how to ask the right questions of my "exhibitors" or prepare the loft for them. Thankfully, one of the first people to respond to my call was Buzz, an enby artist who had been working for the last year as a gallery assistant but was moving into curating. Together, we developed parameters for the exhibit makers and figured out where in the loft we'd put things. We said no to nothing, and soon we had more than twenty-five exhibits planned. Some were small, like a scale model of the Stonewall Inn made from gingerbread (complete with edible cops). Some were huge, like a hand-illustrated, idiosyncratic timeline of queer American history that snaked along the floor of the entire loft. The bathroom was transformed into the "queer women of the blues lounge," with a playlist playing and a binder of information on the singers and songs. Several PhD students turned their dissertations into performance art pieces, and a few playwrights brought in scenes they were working on, so our friends Davi and Ariel agreed to be the MCs for a performance break in the middle of the night. My brother Jim and a mutual friend from our hometown, Tom, volunteered to man the bar—Tom had donated a case of champagne.

Finally, at 8 p.m. on January 10, 2011, we opened the doors on the first-ever Pop-Up Museum of Queer History—and realized we'd made a tremendous mistake. QuORUM had estimated 100 guests over the course of the evening; we had that many people packed in by 9 p.m., and no one was leaving. Some showed up with exhibits they'd never told us about, so after a quick chat with the neighbors on our floor (a bunch of musicians and an up-and-coming theater), we spread throughout the hallways. In the end, nearly 400 people showed up that night. I'd imagined something like a gallery opening with dancing afterward; this was more like a rave inside a museum. The crowd was hot, smart, and messy; more than one of the exhibits came away stained with cup rings. There were moments when I felt like I was walking through a kaleidoscope, with partial, fractal reflections of myself appearing in every face I saw.

It wasn't just me, I realized; people were hungry for queer history and queer space. All of us Gen Xers and Millennials had grown up being told we lived in a "better" time—at least it wasn't the '80s; at least it wasn't the '50s. We should be thankful. We had *Will & Grace*, the sitcom where a straight actor played the straightest gay guy ever, along with his best friend, Jack-the-Walking-Gay-Joke (we all knew Sean Hayes, the actor playing Jack, was gay, but he didn't come out officially until he was forced to in 2010, years after the show was off the air). Madonna, Britney, and Christina Aguilera had pretended to kiss at the MTV Movie Awards. Don't Ask, Don't Tell had finally been repealed (well, for gay troops; trans people were still shit outta luck), and we could get married in a whopping six and a half states (Massachusetts, Connecticut, California, New Hampshire, Iowa, Vermont, and DC)! But tolerance doesn't feed the soul, and our "wins" all focused on making *us* more like *them*. We wanted art, magic, and excellence; we wanted to transcend our present by celebrating our past, every fag or trannie or dyke who'd gotten us this far. We didn't just stand on the shoulders of giants; we wanted to dance on them.

And it seemed perhaps the pendulum had begun to swing back. We'd explored assimilation, seen the good and the bad, and now young queer people were ready to re-embrace strategic separatism on our own terms. We weren't forced into a gay ghetto; we had created a space that straight people (thankfully) avoided.

Then some of them showed up . . .

Around midnight, as we were setting up an exhibit by performance artist Hadassah Damien (life-size cop dolls made of felt, at which people threw high-heeled shoes while screaming the names of their femme ancestors), I noticed a persistent thudding. A weird energy suddenly swirled through the crowd—all the stoners smoking over by the dioramas of Samuel R. Delany novels were stuffing out their joints; someone was yelling by the front door. It could only mean one thing: The cops were here.

I'd spent my life watching the police break up parties—gently, when it was my family at Christmas and Officer Petey was embarrassed to let us know the neighbors had been complaining; or in an impotent fury, like when they tried to shut down our 2003 Valentine's Day party at 2 a.m. and my roommate Rebecca stood up and drunkenly declared, "I am a queer Black Latina Jew working for the ACLU Racial Justice Project. *I shall* handle this" (and she did). Priority number one was always *keep the cops outside*.

I sprinted to the front door, which my roommate Jon was holding mostly closed, preventing the cops from slipping in.

"Sorry," I mouthed at him, then pushed my way out into the hall, which was chockablock with police. My sudden emergence surprised them, and I had time to lock the door and yank it shut behind me. I told them I was in charge and could explain everything if we could just step outside, where it was quieter. They put me in a cruiser while my friend Quito took photos—half evidence in case anything went wrong, half glamour shots to make me look cool as fuck later—and Jon got everyone out the back door of the building.

The cops—annoyed and confused—started asking about underage drinking, and after a tense few minutes where I thought I was being set up, we all realized they were at the wrong address. They'd been trying to bust an under-eighteens punk show they'd read about on Facebook and had gotten confused when they saw all the hubbub outside our building, mistaking our twinks and transmascs for wayward adolescents. They gave me a summons anyway (fire code violation), but then they were gone, leaving just a great origin story in their wake.

The next morning, I put the loft back together to the gentle sound of email endlessly pinging—a virtual flood of messages asking when the next Pop-Up would be, offering to make an exhibit, or wondering if we'd do one in Philly or Boston. I'd imagined the Pop-Up Museum as a provocation, not an organization . . . but why not? Buzz said they were down to take another crack at it. Out of nowhere, a divinity student named Graham appeared with an offer: He was a professional fundraiser for queer nonprofits; he'd handle our finances if we in turn taught him queer history. The Leslie Lohman Foundation for Gay and Lesbian Art (a gallery in Manhattan) agreed to lend us their space in August, when they were typically closed. Suddenly, we had seven months to do our best Mickey Rooney and Judy Garland impressions and Put On A Show.

We created a core collective and, via a long consensus process, developed a few basic priorities: All exhibitors would be paid (even if only nominally); we wouldn't repeat exhibits (the lack of a canon was one of the strengths our history had gained in its years outside mainstream institutions); and all of our shows would be developed collaboratively with the local community (no one likes a carpetbagger who shows up to tell you what you already know, or "should" know).

I looked up one day and it was late spring, and I hadn't thought about leaving in months.

The Pop-Up Museum snapped all the disparate pieces of my life together. A friend from grad school gave us a big initial donation and let us use his apartment for a highfalutin fundraising event. When we ran out of wine at our next opening because 800 people showed up, my dad handed Graham his credit card to go buy more. And when we ran out *again*, my mom did the same. A faerie I met in Tennessee connected me with the archive at the LGBT center he managed in Philadelphia, and they volunteered to host our next show. The aftershocks of the financial crisis were still in the air, and it was easy to find free or cheap space if that was all you needed.

But nothing felt as good as reconnecting with the queer youth center I had worked at a decade before, which had over the years (like me) grown and changed—re-embracing its roots and the youth it had briefly tried to push away, unfucking what I had unwittingly helped fuck up.

When I was trying to be a journalist, I'd gotten the opportunity to do a reported TV spot for Logo, the queer cable channel that would one day launch *Drag Race*. I wasn't good at it, and I wasn't invited back. But I covered a show of monologues by queer women, one of whom—Heather Acs—I'd stayed in touch with through the years. At the first Pop-Up, she'd taken over a large closet and transformed it into a nest, inside which she performed passionate monologues about her history as a queer, working-class Latina from West Virginia. Now, she was working as a part-time arts educator at that same center. For the next Pop-Up, she proposed a one-day all-youth fashion show, where they would be the designers, models, and MCs, and in the process of prepping for it, she would teach them about the queer history of fashion.

Delighted by this idea, I reached out to Luna, the photographer who ran the darkroom at the center (who taught me how to serve face many years ago, when he was the overall father of the House of Khan). He and his students contributed a haunting exhibit of photos that called attention to the invisibility of HIV-positive youth of color, in which the kids in white faceless masks appeared in everyday positions, riding the subway or sitting on playground equipment. Some of the models in the fashion show wore the masks as well, bringing the one-day event and the monthlong exhibit into conversation.

The fashion show was the most popular one-night event we ever did (aside from our openings), with over 200 youth and their families in attendance. Soon after, we developed a collaboration with the center and the City University of New York, creating a semester-long training program for K–12 teachers who wanted help writing queer-positive curricula. I couldn't fix the mistakes I'd made, but it was stupid to let guilt keep me from going back and doing better.

Speaking of which: Being back in Brooklyn reminded me of why I'd left and the wreckage I'd made of my friendship with Brian. While in New Orleans, I'd drink about it frequently, sending him stupid texts that never said anything I really wanted to say. At least, I think that's what I did. I never looked back at my messages, too afraid of my unsettled heart. He'd respond kindly, but at a remove, and I figured I had yet again stretched a friendship past its breaking point.

There had always been something akin in us though; a twinned thing that made people ask if we were brothers even though he was tall and blond, and I, short and dark-haired. He was overly honest (sometimes caustically so), whereas I lied easily, at times reflexively. But we both had a knack for making things happen, whether it was pushing a night until it got weird or escaping the city for Puerto Rico. And we both slipped seamlessly though this new world—pretty White faggots, angry decorative objects. We loved nerdy gay things, especially documentaries, and often found ourselves giving long monologues on esoteric pieces of history to men who only wanted to sleep with us. Perhaps more than anything though, we were united by the Nineties anger we carried, which I now think was created in the gap between what we were told and what we experienced. The straight world expected us to be thankful for the crumbs they tossed us.

We'd rather starve, and we held that hunger like a knife.

Brian's anger was cold and distant, like outer space, capable of freezing an entire room into silence; mine was hot, volcanic, and always, when it finally exploded out of me, loud. He brought out all those familiar feelings in me: I didn't know if I wanted to date him, *Single White Female* him, or go on a killing spree with him.

Around the time I returned to Brooklyn, he'd reached out from Brazil with an idea to sync ourselves again: We'd each do an hour of research a day, on any topic that grabbed us that morning, and we'd email each other a summary.

Yes, our friendship came with homework.

All real ones do, honestly, of one kind or another. It was a bridge to forgiveness, but it was not forgiveness itself. The moral of every story starts at its origin, and this time it was my mistake to fix; my parents taught me that.

Now Brian and I were both back in New York, circling each other warily. Or maybe it was all in my head. God knows I didn't talk to him about it; I just prayed things would magically return to how they were. I wasn't in love with him anymore—I had, at the same time I started Pop-Up, begun a relationship that was already rearranging my life. But decoupling that one element from everything else helped me understand how much I *did* love him, as a near-brother, a queer brother; as the person I wanted to bounce every idea off of and then get tipsy with and go shopping. He was my best friend, the thing I'd spent so much of my life wanting, I'd poisoned every opportunity to have it.

One Sunday, as planning was underway for the second Pop-Up show, he and I ended up accidentally alone—we were heading from *somewhere* to *somewhere else*, and the other people with us had left, or maybe they'd been too slow, but it was now just the pair of us walking together across the Long Meadow in Prospect Park. It was a bright, warm sunny day in June, and Brian was radiating fury. You know that scene in *The Day After Tomorrow*, when the ice age chases Jake Gyllenhaal down a hallway, freezing everything as it goes? I was Jake and Brian was the ice.

I was monologuing about Pop-Up planning, filling the air until someone else was there to alleviate the tension, when Brian interrupted.

"Why didn't you invite me?" he asked bitterly.

I was giving an excuse about him being away, and Pop-Up just sort of . . . *happening*, when I noticed his posture: angled away from me, head down, shoulders forward, eyes narrowed. It was the way I stood near my parents when I was in college, a torqued, concave body position that seemed designed to hide the heart. The only reason my relationship with them had been salvaged was that my mother apologized, unprompted, and then lived up to that apology. My parents had become two of my fiercest allies and closest friends, and if I wanted that with anyone else, I needed to follow in their footsteps.

This was and wasn't about Pop-Up, I knew; just as it was and wasn't about his ex. It was about *us*, and more specifically, it was about me being someone that he trusted, and then hurting him unexpectedly. It was about me being an emotional idiot, and if I was going to stay still—if I was going to run a museum collective—if I was going to have a real relationship, or a best friend, or any future—I needed to start unfucking things.

"I'm sorry," I said, something I'd written in texts (I think) but never really said to his face. "Do you *want* to be involved?"

Brian mulled this over. He was still angry—would be for months, reasonably—but this response surprised him. We talked more, and he ticked off all the reasons he *didn't* want to be involved, and I agreed with all of them. I told him the truth: I wanted him there, but I was too scared to say it, and so I put the onus on him, and that was shitty of me. He melted a little. Enough. We kept walking, and I don't remember the rest of the day, so we must have had fun, though he didn't end up getting involved with that show, and this was not the last of the apologies I needed to give him. It was a step in the right direction, the necessary first one from which all others could flow.

Two years later, I got a grant from the New York Public Library to research the queer history of Brooklyn. By this point, the Pop-Up collective had realized that our exhibitions worked best when they delved deeply into the *local* queer history of wherever we were. We'd missed an opportunity with our first show, so we planned a triumphant Brooklyn homecoming—only to discover that no one really knew much about the queer history of Brooklyn, and so very few people proposed exhibits. It was a strange hole in the otherwise seemingly well-documented history of queer New York. As I thought about it, I realized that *I* didn't know anything about Brooklyn's history either, queer or otherwise.

The show we planned got caught up in institutional politics at a Brooklyn museum that offered us space and then retracted at the last minute, and we had to shelve most of our ideas. But I couldn't stop thinking about this history mystery. Why *didn't* we know about queer Brooklyn? Consumed by this question, I applied for a research fellowship at the New York Public Library in 2015. When I got the money, the head archivist said that by the time the grant period was over, I should have a book proposal completed.

Me, write a book about Brooklyn—the very thing I didn't know anything about? Yes, he said. Soon I'd *be* the expert, wouldn't I?

What would I want out of a book like that, I wondered. It had to be rigorous, of course; there was already enough bad bullshit about queer people out there. It had to be equal to Brooklyn itself—as diverse, as big, as bold; as exciting and important and idiosyncratic. And it couldn't just be an encyclopedia of antique homosexuals. *Here a faggot, there a faggot* might have felt revolutionary in middle school, but I wanted more now. I wanted to understand us: Why were we *here* and not *there*? Why did we use *this word* in *that time*? I'd already seen so much change in queer lives, just in the last three decades: the long arc of the AIDS crisis, the rise and coming dominance of gay marriage, the explosion of ideas about what it means to be trans. I wanted to trace those changes back, to understand *how* we were *who* we were. And I wanted it all to be emotional, moving, and full of ancestors rendered so vividly you'd walk away feeling like they were your own grandparents. Now that I knew I had a future, I wanted a past too—and I wanted to pass that on to the generations below me. I was worried that our Obama-gay-marriage-hopey-kumbaya moment was like a hit of poppers—heady but brief—and that in the aftermath we'd find ourselves spun out: harangued in the public square yet again, but without our private worlds to fall back into. I was becoming history, I realized, and I could either disappear or write myself into the record.

Frankly, what I wanted to do felt impossible.

And it felt exciting. It felt like an adventure, and I knew Brian was the person I needed by my side. He was the only one I knew who could skewer me on my bullshit *and* discuss nineteenth-century sexologists at length. Plus, he liked to drive, and I hated cars, and it turned out, we'd spend the next *five years* traveling to archives around the country to look at dusty correspondence files and rare books that had never seen a scanner. I paid him what I could, when I could, but it would never be enough for all the work he did. We rebuilt our friendship on road trips and treasure hunts; days spent debating *What was the structure of the New York City court system in 1912?*

By the time *When Brooklyn Was Queer* came out in 2019 (right on the fiftieth anniversary of the Stonewall Riots), Brian was well on his way to becoming a professional archivist, and I was already working on my next book, the history of the forgotten women's prison that made Greenwich Village queer. I couldn't have written either of them without Brian. Or without the Pop-Up Museum; without Kendall and the queer youth center; without my parents and brothers; without every bit of my *own* history, the very history I had spent so long wanting to forget. But the only way the past can hurt us is when we deny it—or more frequently, when we are denied access to it.

I had spent years running from the past, both my personal experiences and the painful legacies of being queer in the twentieth century. But when I finally turned to face those memories, they weren't chasing me—they were just there, waiting for me to make sense of them.

A Home at the Beginning of the Apocalypse

No one was home when I unlocked the apartment door, but still, something was wrong. Nine years in a space, and you get to know its subtlest tells—the way sound echoes off or is blunted by the furniture or the warmth of the floor in that one spot, at 11 a.m., after it's been in the sun all morning. I stood in the doorway, keys in hand, trying to sense what had changed.

Boots, the Bed-Stuy alley cat we'd rescued in 2015, shortly after we moved in, yowled at me from the stairs to the basement. He was the sweetest little liar, a real talker, who'd have you convinced every night at nine that he'd never had dinner, not once, not ever. He'd mostly domesticated himself, appearing one afternoon in our backyard, and then returning every night thereafter, until one day, Jason just picked him up. In the winters, late at night, when Jason and I were asleep, Tim would put on a thick smoking robe and go out and let Boots curl up in his lap while he doomscrolled. Then one day Boots showed up with a half-broken leg, so we moved him inside—somewhat against his will—and he was still a little salty about it.

I could sympathize, I frequently told him, but it was dangerous out there for an alley cat alone, and getting more so every day.

Mrrrraaaaaawwwwwww, Boots yelled again, clearly frustrated. I walked over, and then I heard it, a rushing wet sound. I flew past him down the steps to find the basement full of water, at least two inches—enough water that a plastic-wrapped pack of toilet paper was bobbing on it like a raft in the ocean, with our new kittenbaby, Shady, sitting on top.

I grabbed a cat in each hand, locked them in the bathroom, and raced back to our basement water world. The tide was nearly past the baseboards, and it was still pouring in from the other room, the part of the basement we shared with the rest of the house. That was new. Usually we flooded from the back door.

Glug glug glug. The water poured, and I panicked. I had to shut off the water—no, I had to get all the wires and plugs off the floor—no, I had to shut off the electricity—no, the water, it was perilously close to—Jason's suitcase! The one from his mama, that had everything that he had left of—Or maybe—

"Mori! Help!" I yelled, paralyzed by panic.

Mori raced down from the second-floor apartment she shared with her girlfriend April, who was out getting dinner with Lulu, who lived on the top floor. Mori was a software engineer with an uncanny understanding of systems, and she immediately grasped the problem—a rusted, busted water heater—and found the valve to shut it off.

"Jeeez," she murmured, looking into our basement, which had already developed that mildew funk I associated with secondhand, waterlogged books, all puffed up and cheap. The tide had surfaced a stunning array of things, and we stared at them in silence: the pink plastic Christmas ornament that belonged to Baby, our imaginary adopted velociraptor daughter; a handful of Tim's dried-out markers, no longer dry but still not useful; the couch from that vintage Barbie Dream House we'd intended to fix up and sell on eBay, but which had become invisible to us and lived on the floor ever since we found it; the bags and bags of beads that my aunt Eileen had been saving for some unknown reason, but had given to Jason, who was now saving them for his own reasons, which were unknown even to him; the kitchen timer I broke the day we got it but was convinced was fixable . . .

On and on it went, the watery detritus, our own personal Great Pacific Garbage Patch.

How had I, a person who spent a decade living out of a backpack, acquired so much stuff? I looked out at the water, and the last fourteen years looked back at me.

Officially, Tim, Jason, and I met in 2010, when they proposed an exhibit for the first Pop-Up Museum: an altar to the Sisters of Perpetual Indulgence, a gorgeous drag mother superior surrounded by stained glass windows and tiny fake candles, which flickered so convincingly that twice during the night I thought it was actually on fire.

They had made several such altars before, gifts for some of the actors Jason worked with on Broadway. Tim was a set designer by training, and Jason, a costumer; together, they made intricate, intimate displays—dolls, dioramas, shrines; a wall of shelves in their tiny Bushwick apartment that was an ever-evolving gallery of "gorgeous, tasteful, little stylish little gorgeous things," as Jason would say in his best Eddie-from-AbFab voice.

Jason had grown up poor in Mississippi, with a crafty, clever mama who could decorate an entire Christmas tree with just a few boxes of red and green Twinings tea bags; Tim grew up part of an old Virginia line that you wouldn't call hoarders, but they had at least one barn full of tchotchkes and furniture going back to the 1800s, ready to be repaired by Tim's dad and shared with whoever needed a chair that year. Together, they could turn anything into something precious (including, it turned out, me).

The truth: We met on a third-tier hookup site, which had terrible UX but was free. But it was hard enough to tell people about our relationship at all, especially since Jason and Tim had just gotten domestic-partnered (they wore the same matching suits to Pop-Up that they did to city hall). In the decade before we met in 2010, they were the embodiment of couple goals in their social circle. This was long before the slew of polyamory memoirs, or the backlash against polyamory memoirs as bourgeois posturing, or the backlash against the backlash as retread, sex-negative bullshit tarted up by a Twitter-level understanding of Marx. The closest thing to poly celebrity back then were the rumors that Will and Jada Pinkett-Smith were in an open relationship, and that was it. We knew couples who occasionally hooked up with other people, usually on vacation, but that wasn't something you *identified* as; it was just something you did (like being gender nonconforming in the '90s). We wanted people to take us as legitimate, and we did what queer people have always done to fit in: tried to seem less dirty and more straight. So we smoothed our meet-slut into a meet-cute as we began, once again, in our thirties, the process of coming out.

The beginning was rough. No one—including us—thought we were possible. Queer history is full of nonmonogamous relationships, but the decades of AIDS and assimilation had tarnished those ways of living. If you were in an "open" relationship, you were a slut, and your relationship was probably on the rocks anyway; if you wanted to live communally, you were naive and probably a college student or trust fund kid who'd never dealt with the real world. The word *polyamory* was only used in academia or on Tumblr; more often than not, well intended people called us "polygamous" instead.

But the real difficulty wasn't the world—it was us. *Me.* This was not my first time at the sidepiece rodeo, and I knew the flavor of the month curdled fast. That's what I liked about it. I could enjoy all the trappings of someone else's relationship—the in-jokes, the great sex, the well-appointed apartment—and then skedaddle. My longest relationship up to that point was still the year I'd spent with Morgan when I was in college, and on my loneliest nights, it felt nice to warm myself by someone else's fire. I didn't often want to be in a relationship—like friendships, they seemed like a lot of work—but fears of being old and alone still bayed at me.

Jason found my weakness, my safe place: words. We were texting each other for weeks before we met. Dirty texts and funny texts and endless stupid texts; so many texts I had to upgrade to an unlimited plan. By the time we met in person, we already had an ease. Tim and I were the same age, and Jason just five years older; we shared all the same references and many of the same wounds. Jason was on his own gender journey too, and Tim was so tongue-tied, he came out to his parents via a letter he left behind when he went back to college for his junior year. These experiences dislocated us from the rest of the world, but they bonded us together. Tim and I often made the same bad dad jokes simultaneously, and we discovered a companionable silence inside which we could do almost anything together and have fun. We teased Jason that he had simply found a spare in case his original boyfriend broke. By almost every measure, they were opposites: Jason was short, and Tim was tall; Jason femme, Tim masc; Jason, "high-spirited and vivacious," Tim, laidback and laconic. I fit snugly in between them on every scale—and still to this day, I take the middle spot in the bed and on the couch when we watch TV.

They'd gotten together in 2001, when Tim was just out of college, gone to grad school together, moved cross-country together (twice), and adopted two cats together; they were an old married couple before either of them turned thirty-five.

Therein lay the problem. It all happened so fast, each step logically following the last until suddenly there were no new steps to take. Elsewhere they would have settled in, settled down, become that small-town gay couple with a perfectly restored Victorian, a knickknack heaven. New York didn't allow that, and there wasn't much option to leave if they wanted to do theater. Every day was a grind with few rewards beyond getting up to do it again. Most of their work in those early days wasn't designing but doing the assistant jobs that made everything run, so they spent years on the other side of an invisible wall, watching the lives they wanted painfully up close. It was that pigeon experiment all over again, only New York was the inconsistent lever, occasionally rewarding them with a good design gig. But the more interesting the work, the less it paid. Late nights, little money, small apartments, no time to make friends; soon they were peck-peck-pecking at each other. I was a welcome distraction—a guest star introduced in their flagging tenth season, Cousin Oliver to their Brady Bunch.

I tried my best to ruin it early on, predicting easy reasons why it wasn't going to work, even as we were having fun. I was a band-aid on their problems, I told myself, and we had our own issues too. Jason had a temper that could match mine, and we'd already had some minor clashes that made us both wary of what could come next, while Tim would shut down like an obstinate teenager, swaddling himself in a sulky refusal that silently absorbed all argument and stayed unmoving. Six months in, I fled to the Dominican Republic with a good friend, took acid, and decided we needed to break up while I was breaking into a chichi resort for some free food. But that move only works if you're immature. Old me just wouldn't have come back, or wouldn't have called if I did. But I'd done some painful, unavoidable growing, and I couldn't imagine looking at my weaselly face in the mirror every day thereafter if I treated them like that. So we talked and fought, tried to be friends, fought again—spent just as much time together-while-apart as we did together-while-together. Inseparable even in separation: That was the surest sign we were cooked.

Look, all the issues were real: I was both a band-aid and a shady flake; they were annoyed with each other and on shaky relationship ground. But our rough edges matched up just right. Fighting with me united them, and telling myself they'd leave as soon as they were in a better place meant I felt like I had an escape hatch. Is any of that emotionally healthy? No, probably not.

Worked for us though.

We figured out that a thrupple is actually four relationships—the three of us together and every possible couplet—and each has its own needs and joys. It's a balancing act that we're surprisingly good at. Our relationship takes up most of our time, yet within that remains variable. A date night might mean Tim and me taking a ten-mile walk, Jason and me playing Mario Kart, all three of us going to visit friends in Queens, or Jason and Tim taking a taxidermy class while I read on the couch. On those nights, part of me is on the date with them—getting photos of the work in progress, imagining what we'll have for dinner—and another part of me is on my own. It's that liminal space, between solitude and community, that I've always looked for. Being a trio in a world mostly built for couples has its difficulties (we keep a list of things that come in sets of three), but it also means we always have a backup plan, another opinion, or a tie-breaking vote.

Plus we get a lot more presents at anniversary time.

One problem proved intractable, however: our stuff. They were trying to run a costume shop and design studio out of an 800-square-foot railroad apartment. Add in two cats and three humans, and even though I traveled light, it was unlivable. For most of 2011 we shared a double bed in Bushwick, such a tight fit we all had to turn over at the same time, like a joke in a cartoon about the Depression.

I didn't realize it, but my living-out-of-a-suitcase days were already dead. Pop-Up came with paperwork, and exhibits people didn't want back after we showed them, and books I needed to read to understand the community we were working with, and on and on and on.

In October 2011, we found our magical unicorn apartment via Craigslist: the ground floor of a brownstone on a one-way short block in Washington Heights, almost twice the size of our current place for only a slight increase, with a humongous bathtub and more closets than I've ever seen in a New York apartment. And it also had . . . well, the ad called it a yard; it was a trash heap ruled by a poison ivy vine as thick as my wrist. To make it usable, I spent weeks clearing the soil of syringes and broken bottles and rusted chains and saws (which came in handy, since there were a few weedy saplings that needed to be removed too).

Together, the three of us planted anything that would grow in the shady, polluted ground—daffodils and ferns and hostas mostly, the tough broads of the floral world. We rescued an old urn from a movie palace from the '50s, which had been used for decades as a cigarette butt can and, as a result, was so toxic, anything we put in it died; so we placed it in the back corner where even the poison ivy fled from it. There was a feral cat park on one side of us and a nosy antique dealer who raised prize roses on the other. It felt like a bizarro-universe sitcom.

The building had been in the owner's family for generations. He was a bit odd—he gave us a fifty-plus-page binder explaining the rules for trash and recycling (the same rules that applied everywhere in NYC, mind you)—but aside from that, he left us alone. The best part? When we signed the lease, he told us he never raised the rent, because he wanted his tenants to stay; we checked with the upstairs neighbors, who said it was true, and they'd been there over a decade. One day, he told us, he'd retire and take over the building; convert it back to the one-family home it was in eighteen-whatever. But that was far down the line.

For a few months after we moved in, I told my parents that Tim and Jason were my roommates. Then I realized I was being dumb, falling back into my oldest patterns because some part of me will always be a scared sixteen-year-old in 1994. I told my brother Jim the truth first, since he had met them already and was gay, so he knew what a thrupple was.

(Sidenote: *Thrupple* is a terrible word. We've auditioned others: *triad, trio, triumvirate, troika*. They all suck. I think *thrupple*'s the worst, but it's the one that stuck.)

In the early 2010s, being in a thrupple was a lot like being queer in the Nineties: A surprising number of people approached us to shyly admit that they also had two partners—two husbands, a boyfriend and a girlfriend, a wife and a best-friend-with-benefits who lived across the street. We started jokingly calling ourselves "the thrupple whisperers." One of us would get a message out of the blue from an old acquaintance or a coworker, suggesting we just "catch up and chat," and we knew before the evening was out we'd be giving them advice on how to make it work. The key, we told everyone, was the same thing we'd learned from coming out the first time: honesty (and a king-sized bed, maybe a queen if you're all into cuddling and don't have pets).

I don't think monogamy is going away soon; it seems pretty popular, even if most people are bad at it. But over the years Tim, Jason, and I have been together, there has been a surge in people living openly with multiple partners, and I can't help but see it as part of the long tail of the queer '90s. Conservatives were wrong to think gay marriage would pollute the sanctity of straight marriage, but decades of debate about who was owed what for their relationships inevitably cast questions on the utility of marriage as a civil institution. As Supreme Court Justice Samuel Alito put it when opposing gay marriage, "Suppose we rule in your favor in this case and then, after that, a group consisting of two men and two women apply for a marriage license?" He was so close to seeing the point, it's impressive that he missed it entirely. Why *shouldn't* our government support any group of people doing the difficult work of caring for each other during this, the beginning of the Anthropocene? It's scary out there, alley cats, and it's getting scarier every day.

But Alito is right that queer people are changing marriage, much as we've changed the rest of the straight world. Generations of older queers have now headed to the altar, and they have brought with them their history as proud gay sluts or communal-minded lesbians permanently entangled in a web of exes. The internet has (again) assisted these changes: After casual exposure to different family structures around the world, it's hard to see monogamous marriage as the golden calf of God-sanctified sex. For decades, I'd been quietly tracking the ways in which assimilation was changing *us*, but now queer people were spies in the house of love, renovating marriage like gay designers adding a sex dungeon to a 1960s suburban split-level. In 2022, the Kinsey Institute did an analysis of recent rigorous studies into nonmonogamy and found that one in six Americans were interested in trying it (about the same as the number of people who own a cat), one in nine Americans already had (about the same as the number of people who've gone to grad school), and the only group more likely than any other to engage in polyamory was "sexual minorities."

Suck it, Alito.

One night in 2012, my brother Jim and I took the train up to Westchester to get dinner with my parents, and afterward, as we sat in the living room, I told them that Jason and Tim were my boyfriends. "Huh," my dad said, and shrugged and smiled; that was it for him.

My mom considered for a moment. I could see her thinking and wondered what she was about to say.

"Do you . . ." she paused. "Do you all . . . share the same bed?"

I laughed. *This* I was prepared for. If you've never come out as being in a thrupple, I can tell you, this is usually one of the first questions.

"Yes!" I said. "But we're getting a bigger one."

My mom nodded thoughtfully and ran a hand through her short blond hair. The wheels were still turning.

"Are you all . . ." Here she paused even longer. She pursed and unpursed her lips several times, trying to find the right words. " . . . *intimate* at the same time?"

"Mom!" I burst out. I could see Jim in the corner of the room, shaking with a mix of horror and repressed laughter. For a moment, none of us said anything, but then I realized it was not a rhetorical question, and my mother was waiting for the answer.

I took a deep breath. My relationship with my family was a joy, a boon, a great gift we had fought to give one another—and here was the downside. We had run the gamut of awful times and great times and come out stronger on the other side. Nothing was off the table. We were real friends, and real friends ask you nosy fucking questions.

"Yes," I told her, studying the carpet carefully. Now I knew how my father felt when he gave me that sex talk at Cornell. "But think carefully how much more information you want."

My mom considered this for a long time. Curiosity and tact warred across her face. My dad, I believe, was attempting to astral-project himself out of the room. Jim had swallowed his tongue and was dying. Finally, my mother sighed.

"You realize this doesn't get you out of having grandkids, right?"

And like that, my parents gained two sons-in-law.

Although my older brother Johnny was not there for this coming out, I have to give him credit—he was well on his way to having kids at this point, and that took the pressure off. I had long since realized that children were not going to happen for me. My life wasn't conducive to them, and I didn't want to change. Tim and Jason didn't want kids. It made me sad for a while—I think I'd have been a great dad—but it was a dull ache I rarely thought much about anymore. And anyway, soon the niblings started to appear. Johnny had two; Tim's sister had three; Jason wasn't in touch with a lot of his family, but he had one close niece, and he got to know her daughters in California via Zoom calls and care packages.

Then, toward the end of our first season, our new sitcom was canceled: Our loopy landlord showed up one day to tell us he'd sold the building. He wrote us an extended lease that locked us in for another two years, but the first thing the new owner said to us—before we even knew her name—was "Your rent is going up." She forced out the upstairs tenant and moved in her son, a friendly dimwit who had a menagerie of animals and a pack-a-day smoking habit, and soon the building's glorious woodwork smelled like a petting zoo on fire.

Our time in the city, we decided, was over. It was getting more expensive every day, and the earnings of three artists only made up about one real-person salary. Jason never loved New

York anyway (though it loved him); Pop-Up was always pulling me away; and Tim was doing more and more theater design around the country. Maybe we'd find a place near enough in the suburbs that we could continue life pretty much as usual, or perhaps one of us (probably Tim) could get a teaching gig at a college in a small city, and we'd finally fix up the Victorian of our dreams—but either way, we were out.

Then April came along.

She and I had been close friends since the early 2000s. We had traveled together, occasionally lived together, and had a disastrous intertangling that involved her wife leaving her for my roommate. Now she had a new girlfriend—Mori, who adorably, she'd met online via World of Warcraft, where they were in the same queer raid group. Mori was from Texas and was moving to New York so they could be together, but April didn't want to live with just a girlfriend ever again. Particularly not a relationship that was so new. They'd vacationed together extensively and spent long visits with each other, but living together is a different beast. So April proposed an idea.

A decade earlier, she'd used a small inheritance to buy her apartment in Park Slope, which had more than tripled in value. She could sell her apartment and use the proceeds for a downpayment on a building, but she couldn't afford the mortgage on her own—and that's why she approached Tim, Jason, Lulu (her college bestie), and me. If we could find the right place, we could each have our own apartments but share the costs and work and joys and fears that come with home ownership.

It took a year of looking before we found the right spot: a rehabbed Brooklyn tenement from 1899 with three separate apartments, plus a shared basement that could be studios for Tim and Jason and a laundry/storage space for the whole house. We'd been on the verge of giving up when Lulu saw the listing—it was out of our price range and advertised as a "luxury renovation," so early in our hunt we wouldn't have bothered to look at it. Thank God we did: The renovation wasn't so much "luxury" as the shiny patina of luxury shellacked over cheap Home Depot materials, and the developers had run into trouble. Their investor needed his money back suddenly and was demanding they sell. They hadn't finished most of the work, but they had written the marketing materials as though the renovation was complete, so all the other prospective buyers were immediately turned off when the apartments were lacking promised bedrooms and the roof was an old sieve, not a high-end deck. We snapped it up for less than the asking price—an unheard of stroke of luck in 2015—and up until the day we signed the contract, the developers were sneaking around for a better deal. But they were stuck with us.

Housing law was not set up for the kind of communal ownership / separate living we imagined. It took five years and three separate lawyers to create a legal structure for our existence. Thankfully, as a group of queers and immigrants, we were used to operating outside the law. History provided us with so many spiritual examples to draw on. When I researched Brooklyn, I came across the Graham Brothers, two men who changed their names, left their families, and lived together as "brothers" (with, for a while, a "sister") as they became important businessmen in New York City in the 1810s. I also found queer communal houses in the 1890s, 1920s, and 1940s, and a veritable explosion of them in the 1970s, after Stonewall ushered in our modern era of visibility. What was the entire world of ballroom, or the squats in Berlin, or the commune in Tennessee but a parallel plane of family existence for its members? For that matter, what was the house I grew up in, if not a collection of people living separate lives communally, often without state protections? The biggest problem with marriage, I came to see, was not just that it denied benefits to relationships of care that deserved them but that it blinded us (and the government) to all the relationships of care *other* than marriage that we were already part of.

Over a series of long brunches, the six of us drew up a thirty-plus-page document that outlined how we'd live together—who owned what, how we'd handle disputes, and who we were relative to each other. We updated our wills and health-care proxies and all the other documents that you need to approximate the legal protections that come automatically when you drunkenly go to Las Vegas and marry someone whose last name you don't know. Queer people have always taken the castoffs of straight culture and repurposed them for our own use. In the arts, this created camp, the two-tongued language of sincere hyperbole and furious laughter. In the law, this built an endless number of work-arounds, like queer folks adopting their lovers as their adult children. And new queer groups are pushing these legal boundaries even further, like the Scarborough family, eight adults and three children whom I interviewed several times right as we were moving into our house. They'd bought a dilapidated mansion in the Connecticut suburbs that was zoned for "single-family usage," and when their neighbors tried to force them out—forcing a limited, hetero definition of "family" on them at the same time—they staked their claim by sighting an archaic legal provision that allowed them to have an unlimited number of "live-in servants."

Adapt or die, Darwin said, and we queers are apex survivors.

The six of us moved in together just as the New York Public Library gave me that grant to research the queer history of Brooklyn. There was a tiny bonus room in our apartment (the broker explained it was technically a second bedroom, as it had a window, but unfortunately the door wouldn't open if you put a twin bed in it). That became my office.

My office.

A space of my own, in a place that I owned. In New York City. A spot where I could see all of my books at the same time and close the door when I needed privacy. Not to be all Virginia Woolf about it, but it made an immeasurable difference in my writing. I don't know if I could have written something as complicated as a book without my tiny library. I know I couldn't have stayed in New York. Every day, in a hundred ways, this bit of stability—this new root—makes my life possible. We were here when Tim's dad got cancer and Jason's father died; when my parents had to sell their house; when the pandemic shut the world down; when Lulu lost her job; when April and Mori's old cat died and they got new kittens; when our oldest cat died, and then when our second-oldest cat died; when Lulu's cat died . . . did I mention, we named our building Cat House? At our cattiest, we had seven indoor ones and three strays that we fed outside.

Shortly after we moved in, we were all sitting together watching the 2016 election as it became clear that Donald Trump had beaten Hillary Clinton. What we had expected to be a fun night of complaining about centrist Dems instead became the first of many quiet, fearful nights wondering what would happen next. Our little commune was as much a fortress as a home, we realized, and when Covid-19 swept in, the safety it offered was a life raft.

What do married people do when they're both sick or if they lose their jobs at the same time? It seems like a lonely life.

When the basement flooded in 2023, it wasn't just Mori who came to our rescue. When April and Lulu got home a little later, they instantly appraised the situation as an absolute clusterfuck, beyond our ability to fix. By 2 a.m., we had a team of hired cleaners sucking out the water, and the next day, everyone helped lay out our sodden stuff on every surface that got some sunlight. With a little sleep and the help of five friends, impossible tasks can become merely annoying.

I didn't set out to create a queer reflection of my childhood home, but my subconscious is strong. In our house now there is just as much care and just as much chaos too. The six of us are bonded together in multitudinous ways: love, history, and in-jokes as much as investments, contracts, and group chats. We bought a car together—a light blue Honda Odyssey, the most suburban of vehicles, which can fit our entire commune snugly. We have a bumper sticker that says, "My other car is an Iliad," and a shared calendar for who's using it on what day. Usually on Thanksgiving we all pack into it to gorge ourselves with my family, though these days, my cousin Kathy hosts the party, not my parents.

But the six of us are separate too, each with our own kitchens, lives, and friends. Frost was right; good fences make good neighbors. We get on each other's nerves sometimes, but the recycling still has to go out on Thursdays. It's a different kind of family from the one my parents built, but I live a different kind of life, in a different era, and this works for me. For all of us, it seems. So far. Take it from a former alley cat: It's scary out there on your own, and getting scarier every day.

Epilogue

IN 2024, MY HOMETOWN HELD AN EVENT WHERE THEY recognized "Irvington elders," including my aunt Kathleen, who had just turned ninety. My family bought two tables' worth of tickets, and a ragtag dozen of us showed up for the honors. I sat next to my cousin Jo, who'd been one of my regular babysitters when we were kids but now was a mom of three young adults, living in suburban Virginia. Her middle kid, June, had just come out as nonbinary and transfeminine, which was something of a surprise for most of the family, but at our Christmas party in 2022 or 2021, we'd locked eyes, and I'd just known they were part of the alphabet mafia.

We always find each other.

Over the years, my parents had become integral to the Irvington community: elected to the town council, running the historical society, sitting on the board of the local Planned

Parenthood. So they kept the event going as Jo and I chatted. In the program, they asked each honoree what changes to our town they were most excited about, and Jo's mom talked about all the pride flags running down Main Street in June, how far we'd all come.

"You know," Jo said to me, "your mother really helped us when June came out."

She told me that they'd been celebrating a new family tradition (bitches weekend, when my aunts and older female cousins share a hotel suite in Miami for a few days), and—deep in the drink, long after they'd stopped sending us videos of my aunts dancing to Pitbull—Jo had asked my mom about June, what they should do.

My mother became serious and urgent and sad: Love them, she said. Listen to them. Don't do what we did.

The event started again, and Jo turned back to watch the stage. I excused myself from the table and cried in the bathroom for a little while, overcome by the rushing of the world, which I could feel spinning beneath and above me, inside and beyond me. None of us in that room were who we had been thirty years ago, and we were all better for it.

A few months later, at Christmas, June, Jo, and I were leaning against the stairwell in my childhood home. June was talking about hormones, and DJing, and some trans icon I was only slightly aware of (June is definitely the coolest person I know). "She's so cunt," they said, and I was shocked by the way the world continued spinning, time still moving forward, Jo's smile unchanged. My heart pounded and then leveled out. No one was going to punish us for being queer here, now.

And then a second shock: June was part of a big underground queer scene in Richmond, Virginia, and the language of my students from Bed-Stuy and Harlem twenty years ago was in their mouth. That new world I watched my students summon?

To paraphrase ACT UP: It's here. It's queer. And it's only getting started.

Writing a book about yourself is a solipsistic endeavor, and there are days where I still feel deeply uncomfortable with it. I'm doing this in large part for the money, because without children or a society that cares for elders, the quality of my old age (if I get one) will depend on the silly little numbers on a screen somewhere that determine how much I am worth. But as much as I want to be an old curmudgeon, I can't help but believe that our personal stories are what change the world.

As a historian, I try to get as close as I can to the experiences of everyday people, to hear their thoughts and understand their struggles and, through them, to document the great weaving of time. And it has occurred to me, as I write this book, that my refusal to tell my own story is a refusal to fully participate in this weaving. It's one more way in which the long tail of the queer '90s has remained alive inside me, that pernicious silence that continually snarls its hands around my throat.

I never did find my way back to the church, but one part of my early Catholic life has always stuck with me: James 2:18, often paraphrased as "You will know me by my work." I've always wanted my *work* to stand in for my *self*—a vestige of personal discomfort, which I think will probably never leave me, like how I hate holding hands with Tim and Jason in public.

As Jason would say, "Cry me a tear pie." I shouldn't have spent thirty years fighting for queer visibility if I didn't want to be seen. When I refuse to talk about what I did wrong, or what others did wrong to me, I make it impossible to see how we changed; how we remade ourselves and, through that work, remade the world. But that is the only story worth telling.

My life mattered because I lived it, and I think it will be most useful to future generations in precisely those moments that were hardest to write, those where I fit the world least. Queer theorist Jose Muñoz wrote that queerness is always on the horizon, never here, because queerness is constitutionally *odd*, out of sync. It can never fully arrive; it is always in the potential of those who do not fit. So perhaps those are the moments when I have been my queerest.

My best.

As I write this, fascism is (again) sweeping into the White House. The gentle tech nerds I met at Burning Man in 1999 are now the horsemen of our digital apocalypse. Covid is *still* running rampant, and taking a page from Ronald Reagan and AIDS, our government has decided not to talk about it. Queer people—especially trans folks, immigrant queers, and queer people of color—are in more danger than we've been since . . . well, the Nineties.

And yet we're still here, and there are more of us every year. According to the latest Gallop polls, only 5 percent of Gen X identifies as queer, as opposed to 21 percent of Gen Z. Something fundamental has shifted in our understanding of sex, gender, and sexuality. These days, I see gender and sexual orientation as parts of a much broader tapestry of desire and identity. Many different paths lead to—and pass through—these labels. They're not fake, but they are limited. The internet has opened us to new ways of knowing and allowed queer people to define ourselves and demand that the world listen. We're inventing new language to describe the new selves we have allowed ourselves to become, creating new genders and new kinds of family as we go. Like poppers spilled at an orgy, we can't be poured back into the bottle we came from.

But those fuckface weasels are trying to anyway.

I believe the future is ours, on the long time scale that Martin Luther King Jr. called the moral arc of the universe. Queer people are a permanent part of the world, but how we express our queerness—how we experience our desires and what we call them—shifts as our culture changes. We are firmly in a new, postinternet era. They can ban pediatric gender transition medicine all they want, but unless they take us back to the 1980s, before cell phones and Wi-Fi, they'll never turn our minds back. And even if they did, there would *still* be queer people. Kill us all they want, straight people inevitably make more queers. It is their fatal flaw; it is their saving grace.

But our present is a war for survival. How do we make it through? How we've always done it: Together when we can and alone when we have to. By finding the ties that nourish us and cutting the ones that hold us down. Through solidarity and autonomy, community and freedom, you and me.

I don't mean that in some arty-farty, #blessed #healing #gratitude kind of way. Real community, just like real freedom, takes hard work. It means showing up for each other, processing your bullshit, and learning to say the hard stuff before it devours you from inside. Inevitably you will fuck up, and so will the people you are closest to, and on that day you'll have to ask yourself what you can forgive and how you can atone. That day will come over and over again, if you live long enough, and you'll spend time on both sides of the equation. That's called learning. It sucks.

But it's necessary.

I used to think the Nineties were the quietest, most boring time to grow up. A frozen capsule of insignificance. But now I think it was an egg, just waiting for us to peck our way out. What a beautiful queer flock we make when we spread our wings together.

Acknowledgments

This book has been a long labor—in some ways expectedly, and in some ways surprisingly. It could not exist without a huge community of people who deserve more thanks than I can ever give in print. But I'll try.

First, to my students and fellow faculty at the Bennington Writing Seminars, who reminded me how much I love personal essays and inspired me to write this book. Thank you for creating a literary world that's big enough to fit this history nerd.

To my early readers, who provided an incredible service helping me to shape these bits of memory and prognostication into essays someone else would want to read: Shawna Kay Rodenberg, Oliver Radclyffe, David Schwartz, Susie Merrell, Michael Waters, Alejandro Varela, Keiko Lane, Joshua Gutterman Tranen, Tim McMath, Jason Bishop, Brian Ferree, and Jim Ryan.

To both my editors, Anu Roy-Chaudhury, for seeing the potential in this book, and Ruben Reyes Jr., for getting it across the finish line. To my agent, Robert Guinsler, for the months spent developing the proposal for this book—and also for selling it!

Most of all, thank you to my family and friends who appear in these pages, the ones who are still with us and the ones who are gone; the ones I'm in touch with and the ones long in my past. All of you made this book possible. I hope I've done right by you.

Credit: M Sharkey

Hugh Ryan is the award-winning author of *When Brooklyn Was Queer* (2019) and *The Women's House of Detention* (2022). He teaches creative nonfiction in the MFA program at the Bennington Writing Seminars and runs the Queer History 101 Book Club with world-famous performer Peppermint. He lives in Brooklyn.